from FREEZER *to* COOKER

DELICIOUS WHOLE-FOODS MEALS for the
Slow Cooker, Pressure Cooker, and Instant Pot

POLLY CONNER & RACHEL TIEMEYER

Photographs by Hélène Dujardin

RODALE.

Published in the United States by Rodale Books, an imprint
of Random House, a division of Penguin Random House
LLC, New York.
rodalebooks.com

RODALE and the Plant colophon are registered trademarks
of Penguin Random House LLC.

Library of Congress Control Number: 2019946276

ISBN 978-1-63565-312-0

Printed in China

Book and cover design by Rae Ann Spitzenberger
Cover and interior photographs copyright © 2020 by
Hélène Dujardin

10 9 8 7 6 5 4 3 2 1

First Edition

To the hardworking parents who make dinnertime around the table happen

CONTENTS

INTRODUCTION

"How can I get dinner on the table tonight?"

From our experience feeding our own families, writing a food blog, and teaching freezer-cooking seminars for many years now, we know this is a looming question you're asking almost every day. Hey, we are, too!

We're guessing you understand the benefits of eating at home. You get just how important it is to look your kids and loved ones in the eye over a meal and talk about your day. You know that home-cooked food with whole-food ingredients is always better for you than eating out or grabbing processed junk from the store. You want to watch your budget and cook from scratch and/or in bulk to save money. 'Cause you're smart like that.

But we also know that no matter how well any of us plans, getting a healthy dinner on the table on a weeknight can be a struggle. Life happens. You leave work later than usual. There's a whiny toddler hanging on your leg. You forget to throw dinner in the slow cooker that morning or to thaw a freezer meal in advance. You're ferrying children to baseball practice or piano lessons all evening. Maybe you're just bone-dead tired.

That's *exactly* why we created this cookbook. With the use of your slow cooker or Instant Pot and your freezer, we're going to help you get a nutritious and delicious dinner on the table each night *despite* what life may throw at you.

This cookbook is truly one of a kind. Out of the thousands of cookbooks on the market, there is nothing—*and we mean nothing*—like it. Every recipe in this book can be made in the slow cooker *or* the Instant Pot. In addition to that, every recipe includes freezing instructions, and most can even be cooked straight from frozen in the Instant Pot. With our recipes in hand, you can prep meals ahead in bulk for virtually hands-free meals down the road.

With two years of recipe development for this book and five hundred volunteer recipe testers on our team (seriously!), we are thrilled to teach you everything we've learned about freezer cooking for the slow cooker and Instant Pot. We truly believe this is going to be an incredibly valuable resource for the busy parent (or college student, or working adult) who values eating wholesome meals at home.

Our recipes are all about versatility. Let's take a look at how our cookbook concept works to help get dinner on the table.

How Can I Get Dinner on the Table?

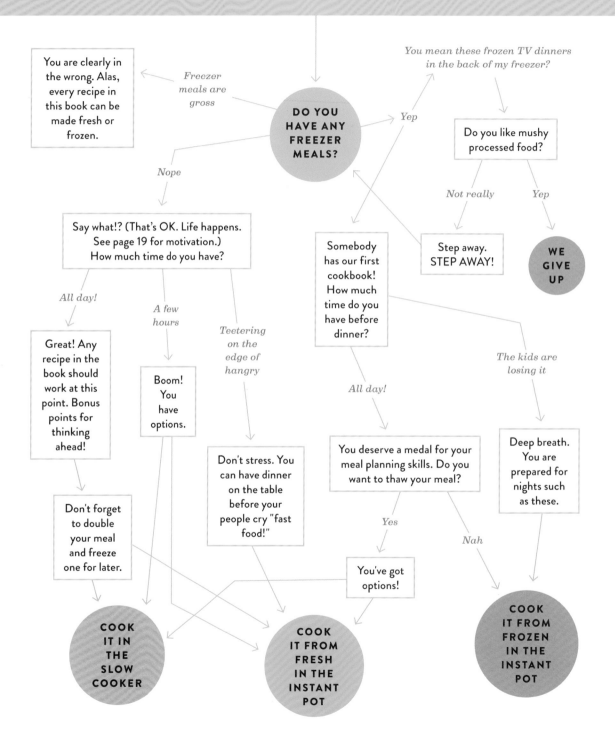

You are clearly in the wrong. Alas, every recipe in this book can be made fresh or frozen.

Freezer meals are gross

DO YOU HAVE ANY FREEZER MEALS?

Yep

You mean these frozen TV dinners in the back of my freezer?

Do you like mushy processed food?

Not really

Step away. STEP AWAY!

Yep

WE GIVE UP

Nope

Say what!? (That's OK. Life happens. See page 19 for motivation.) How much time do you have?

All day!

Great! Any recipe in the book should work at this point. Bonus points for thinking ahead!

Don't forget to double your meal and freeze one for later.

A few hours

Boom! You have options.

Teetering on the edge of hangry

Don't stress. You can have dinner on the table before your people cry "fast food!"

Somebody has our first cookbook! How much time do you have before dinner?

All day!

You deserve a medal for your meal planning skills. Do you want to thaw your meal?

Yes

The kids are losing it

Deep breath. You are prepared for nights such as these.

You've got options!

Nah

COOK IT IN THE SLOW COOKER

COOK IT FROM FRESH IN THE INSTANT POT

COOK IT FROM FROZEN IN THE INSTANT POT

ABOUT OUR RECIPES

When we dove into creating recipes for this book, we had no idea we had signed up for one big tasty science experiment. Using our meat thermometers as our guide, we honed in on the perfect cooking times for all of our freezer-friendly recipes that your family will be making in the slow cooker or Instant Pot over and over again.

As we created and developed an arsenal of amazing recipes, we worked hard to make sure all of them met these five goals:

Goal #1
DELICIOUS.

We aren't here to waste anyone's time. If a recipe wasn't one that our own families and our recipe-testing team enjoyed, it simply didn't make the cut. Like you, if we're going to spend time cooking, we want some yummy food on the table! So deliciousness was our first and most important goal.

Goal #2
CAN BE MADE IN BOTH THE SLOW COOKER AND THE INSTANT POT.

Every recipe in this book has instructions for cooking the dish in the slow cooker and the Instant Pot (or another electric pressure cooker). We worked hard to perfect the cooking times for each of these cookers to ensure you aren't overcooking (or undercooking) your food.

Goal #3
FREEZER-FRIENDLY.

Although every recipe in here was created and tested as a fresh meal, it also had to pass the freezer-friendly test. That means it must freeze, thaw, and prepare successfully, with no major textural or taste changes along the way. To make it easy for you, we've included simple freezer meal instructions at the bottom of every recipe.

Goal #4
WHOLE FOODS.

What makes our recipes stand out from freezer meals you might find elsewhere is that they are primarily made with whole-food ingredients. Each one reflects our commitment to the "whole-foods philosophy," where cooking at home, carefully selecting all-natural ingredients, and eating a variety of vegetables and fruits, whole grains, healthy fats, and local or organic meats are the foundations of a healthy diet.

Goal #5
EASY TO PREPARE.

If you're reading this book, we know you have a packed schedule. As much as you may love cooking (or not), your time is precious. So we've intentionally chosen recipes that are simple enough for anyone to make. We tried to find the shortest path to the best result in every single one.

HOW TO USE OUR RECIPE ICONS

Throughout the book, we've included icons to guide you to recipes that meet your specific needs and lifestyle. To easily find these recipes, consult the Recipe Icon Index on page 244.

Gluten-Free
"Gluten-free" doesn't have to mean taste-free. We've flagged many great options that will not only make your gluten-free eater happy, but are sure to satisfy everyone else at the dinner table as well.

Dairy-Free
Whether you're lactose-intolerant or just want to cut back on your dairy intake, these are dairy-free recipes you won't want to miss.

Vegetarian
Get your greens on! All these recipes are veggie-based, filling, and packed with flavor.

Drop-and-Go
Our definition of a drop-and-go recipe is that it has no precooking requirements and minimal steps at the end. While most drop-and-go meals tend to lack flavor and texture, we've ensured that our recipes have lots of both!

Kid Favorite
Got a picky eater on your hands? Want a meal that you know kids will gobble up with no complaints? We've got your back. We've gone through and identified the recipes that have proven to be no-fail meals for children.

Slow Cooks All Day
Let the slow cooker do the work all day and come home to these mouth-watering meals waiting for you. Every meal with this icon will cook for at least 8 hours.

Feeds a Crowd
Expecting company? Have a large family to feed? These recipes make at least eight servings.

Fully Cook and Freeze
We've identified recipes that can be fully cooked and frozen in individual portions or as a full meal. These are great to reheat for lunches or as smaller meals for singles, empty nesters, college students, or the elderly. Jump to page 19 to quickly learn the best way to freeze and rewarm your fully cooked meals.

It's almost time to get dinner on the table! But first, let's take a few minutes to make sure you understand the basics of your slow cooker or Instant Pot. We promise we'll make it as painless as possible.

slow cooker basics

Slow cooking is a no-brainer, right? Well, we thought so, too. That is, until we began testing recipes for this cookbook. We discovered that many of our underlying assumptions about slow cooking were off. The good news is, after our countless recipe tests, we've learned some key guidelines that will help you make home run meals in the slow cooker every time.

THE 10 COMMANDMENTS OF SLOW COOKING

1. Know thy slow cooker.

For many years, I (Polly) used a bad slow cooker. What I mean by this is, it cooked my food way too hot. It dried out *everything* I cooked in it. It wasn't until I began testing recipes for this cookbook that I realized I was working with a dud. This is why it's so important to know thy slow cooker! With dozens of models on the market, not all slow cookers are created equal. Some models run hot and fast, while others heat more slowly and gently. The only way to find out where yours falls is by experience. Because you likely have a different model of slow cooker than we do, we've provided a range of cooking times in our recipes. **Check your meal's doneness at the lower end of the cooking range.** For example, for a 5- to 7-hour cooking time, check for doneness at 5 hours. After that, check the meal every 30 minutes.

It's worth noting that all our recipes were tested with a KitchenAid 6-quart slow cooker, which was America's Test Kitchen's number one recommended slow cooker at the time of this book's publication. Our suggested cooking times have been built around the results that this appliance yielded. We definitely recommend this one, but most slow cookers will do the task. *Note:* We don't recommend using the slow cooker function on the Instant Pot, since it cooks differently and results may vary.

2. Use thy meat thermometer.

We've found that there are a wide variety of opinions when it comes to how long meals should be cooked in the slow cooker. Because of this, we determined "doneness" by measuring the internal temperature on those recipes that are easy to overcook and dry out (i.e., chicken, pork, and egg dishes). Numbers don't lie. **A meat thermometer will become your best friend when using a slow cooker.** Let it be your guide instead of the clock, and you'll be amazed at how great food can be when it's cooked perfectly. For additional information on safe internal temperatures, see our reference chart on page 249.

3. A few extra steps giveth more flavor.

While we do offer a good amount of the highly requested drop-and-go meals (see page 245 for a list of them), most cooker recipes take just a wee bit more effort to end up with a meal that you'll love. Our number one goal is to provide you with *delicious* recipes. To achieve that goal, we found that most of the time, flavor and texture need to be developed on the front end or on the back end. We worked hard to keep recipes as simple as possible and included as many shortcuts as we could. You'll have to trust us, though, when we say **slow cooker meals taste much better when you take an extra step or two,** such as sautéing aromatics at the beginning, broiling at the end, or thickening a sauce with a cornstarch mixture.

4. Thou shalt not cook frozen food in the slow cooker.

Sorry to be the bearers of bad news, but while cooking a frozen meal in the Instant Pot is safe, putting a frozen meal in the slow cooker is not generally recommended. Loading your slow cooker with icy ingredients will keep food in the temperature danger zone (40° to 140°F), where bacteria can flourish, for too long.

We recommend that you always thaw your meals before putting them in the slow cooker. It's just not worth the risk. Learn the four safe ways to thaw frozen food on page 23.

5. Many meals cook much faster than thou thinketh.

Most of us love the idea of a meal cooking all day while we're away working or out and about. We do, too! In fact, we've identified all our "Slow Cooks All Day" recipes on page 246. However, the cooking times in many online recipes (and even some in cookbooks) will result in overcooked food. This is especially true when it comes to chicken recipes. While some of our cooking times may seem shorter than you're used to, **we can assure you that they are based on rigorous testing of safe internal temperatures, not our preference.** So yes, we'd love for all our recipes to be all-day slow cooker meals, but the truth is that many simply won't turn out well if left to cook for long periods. Our end goal is a great meal, so we worked hard to find the ideal cooking times for every recipe.

6. Keep thy lid closed.

Each peek you take during the cooking process will add 15 to 20 minutes to the cooking time. So curb the urge to open the lid and stir, *unless* we specifically instruct you to. It's usually not necessary and tends to slow down the cooking. It's hard, we know!

7. Thou shalt use the Low heat setting when possible.

While some recipes do give the option of low- or high-heat cooking, **low and slow is always your best bet.** A general rule of thumb is that cooking on the Low setting takes about twice as long as cooking on High. High is only recommended for recipes that take at least 8 hours on Low, however. Anything shorter than that will not do well on the High setting. We do not recommend *ever* cooking chicken on High, for instance. This will lead to a dried-out chicken dinner.

8. Toss thy food if thy cooker was not activated.

Forgot to turn on your cooker (or accidentally tried to "cook" your meal on the Warm setting)? Been there, done that. Any food that sits in your slow cooker or Instant Pot between 40° and 140°F for more than 2 hours is in the perfect environment for bacteria growth. Toss it, shed a tear, and start again.

9. Thou shalt adjust the cooking time for high altitudes.

Well, hello, up there! For high-altitude cooking—roughly 3,000 feet above sea level—add an additional 30 minutes for each hour of time specified in the recipe.

10. Thou shalt enjoy the fruits of thy labor.

Slow cooker meals are a low-stress way to get a delicious dinner on the table on even the busiest nights. Our hope is that our recipes free you up to be relaxed and present with the people you love most, over good food and conversation.

instant pot basics

You have questions. We have answers! Because the Instant Pot hasn't been around as long as the slow cooker, we'll take a bit more time to answer the common questions we've heard again and again. We can't cover every question in this section, but we do want to hit the top ten. *Note:* We've chosen to focus on the Instant Pot, which is the most popular electric pressure cooker on the market, but most of this information will apply across brands.

Before we hit the Q&As, it's important to know that using an Instant Pot is part art and part science—even more so when cooking freezer meals in it. (Type A personalities, we can feel you cringing!) There's definitely a learning curve and, honestly, some necessary trial and error before you'll feel entirely comfortable with this appliance. Once you get a bit of practice, though, you'll gain confidence and intuition when using it. Look on the bright side! We've taken out a lot of the guesswork by providing well-tested recipes and all the basic info you need to get started on the right track.

TOP 10 INSTANT POT QUESTIONS

1. "What the heck *is* an Instant Pot?"

An Instant Pot is the most popular brand of what's called a multicooker. It's an electric countertop appliance that has several cooking functions. It can work as a pressure cooker (which is how we'll mainly use it in this book), slow cooker, steamer, yogurt maker, sauté pan, rice cooker, and/or warming pot, depending on which model you purchase. As new models come out, its features continue to evolve and expand.

2. "Do I really need an Instant Pot?"

If you're wondering whether to invest in an Instant Pot, you may want to consider some of the advantages it offers:

▸ *Cooks food fast.* Well, faster than the normal time, anyway. It can actually cook many dishes up to 70 percent faster, which works particularly well for thick meats, beans, and stocks. We also find ourselves reaching for it almost daily to quickly make healthy soups, hard-boiled eggs, steamed rice, and even freezer meals that we forgot to put in the slow cooker earlier in the day. That's right! If you miss the window for your slow cooker, the Instant Pot and our instructions in each recipe are right there as your fail-safe. (Keep in mind that the total cook time for an Instant Pot meal is a little longer than it may appear, since you must include the time it takes to build pressure, cook the food, and then release the pressure.)

▸ *Cooks food directly from frozen.* Since the USDA states that it's not safe to cook frozen meals in the slow cooker, the Instant Pot is a great solution. If you take some time to prep meals ahead and freeze them, dinner can be as simple as plopping that frozen block in the Instant Pot, pushing a few buttons, and kicking back while it does its magic. See our tips on page 20.

▸ *Fewer dishes.* The Instant Pot truly is a one-pot wonder, meaning you don't have to use multiple appliances and dishes to get the job done. Check this out: You can sauté your aromatics (like onions, garlic, celery, etc.) or sear your meat right in the same pot that you will then quickly pressure cook your meal in. Need to thicken a sauce at the end of a meal? Just stir in a cornstarch mixture and use the Sauté function to simmer until thickened. Then store any leftovers in the fridge in the same pot, and toss it in the dishwasher when they're gone.

▸ *Environmentally friendly.* With a faster cooking time and an efficient use of energy, electric pressure cookers are eco-friendly. When compared with stovetop and other cooking methods, pressure cooking uses two to three times less energy. That saves money on your electric bill, and as a bonus, the Instant Pot can be used in the summer as a great indoor-cooking option in place of the oven.

▸ *Cooks safely.* The stainless-steel pot is one of the safest materials to cook in, avoiding toxic nonstick coatings, aluminum, lead, and more elements that can contaminate your food.

3. "Help! I'm paralyzed by choice. What should I look for when buying an electric pressure cooker?"

When shopping for a pressure cooker, you may be overwhelmed by the *many* different Instant Pot versions and other brands of electric pressure cookers on the market.

The important thing to know for this book is that we tested all our recipes in a 6-quart Instant Pot. Make sure to see our tip for using an 8-quart cooker under Question #5.

According to America's Test Kitchen, the Instant Pot brand of pressure cooker does tend to cook slightly faster and hotter than the other brands they tested. So while you're welcome to use whatever brand you want, you'll get the most accurate results if you use an Instant Pot for our recipes.

To allow for variability between types of electric pressure cookers, **we created our recipes to only use three general functions on your cooker.** (Each pressure cooker's exact button names will vary.)

▸ *Sauté*—We use this function (on its highest setting) in several recipes to precook veggies and sometimes sear meat to kick-start amazing flavor.

▸ *Pressure Cook*—All our recipes will have you manually select how long your meal will pressure cook at "high pressure." Forget those preset buttons for "Soup," "Poultry," etc. We've found that they're likely to overcook your food.

▸ *Cancel*—This button will turn off any cooking function.

4. "My Instant Pot is still in the box. I'm too scared to use it! How do I start?"

Hundreds of thousands of people have become devotees of the Instant Pot, and for good reason. After a short setup and learning curve, *anyone* can use this device. It may look intimidating, but you can do it! The hardest part (which isn't that hard at all) is pulling it out of the box and skimming the manual. Just set aside about 30 minutes to get your amazing new cooker up and running—or better yet, do it right now! You'll be so glad you did.

The owner's manual can seem over-whelming. Here are the four main things to read about in your manual and to practice:

1 Study the parts of your cooker and practice how they fit together. Pay special attention to how the sealing ring should fit snugly inside the lid. (This has been our most common mistake in our own use!)

2 Make sure you understand how to use the three basic functions we listed in Question #3. Ignore the rest for now.

3 Read about how to release the pressure when you're done cooking a meal. There are two ways: natural release and quick release. (See Question #8 to learn more.)

4 Perform an initial test run using water, which your manual will walk you through. This is optional but recommended to help you become familiar with your pot and make sure it's working properly. It only takes about 15 minutes.

Now, start off with a bang! A great first recipe to try would be either the Vegetarian Tortilla Soup (page 199) or Fiesta Lime Chicken Bowls (page 63). Both are drop-and-go meals that won't take long, are hard to mess up, and are yummy!

5. "How much liquid does my Instant Pot need to cook a recipe?"

An Instant Pot requires steam, and therefore liquid, to come to pressure. All our recipes—which were tested in a 6-quart Instant Pot—have accounted for this and include at least 1 cup of liquid in some form (broth, salsa, water, etc.). If you're using an 8-quart cooker, make sure there is at least 1½ cups of liquid. The liquid needs to be a thin, watery consistency (not oil-based).

6. "How long does it take for the Instant Pot to come to pressure?"

In order for your cooker to work, it needs time to build pressure inside the pot. How long this takes depends on the temperature and volume of the food in the Instant Pot and the size of the Instant Pot itself. Think about how long it takes something to come to a boil on the stove; it's typically about the same amount of time to build pressure in a cooker. For fresh meals, assume roughly 10 to 15 minutes, sometimes more, sometimes less. When cooking meals from frozen, it takes almost double the amount of time, usually 20 to 30 minutes. For some of our frozen meals, we'll first instruct you to cook them in the Instant Pot for 5 minutes using the Sauté function. This step releases some liquid and speeds up the process of coming to pressure.

7. "How long does it take to pressure cook a meal?"

See our cooking times chart on page 251 for general recommendations. While we specify a cooking time in every recipe, you might need to adjust it depending on your ingredients or even your altitude (see Question #11). You don't need to increase the time for volume of food, but you may need to adjust for density. What we mean is if a cut of meat is larger or smaller than the one specified in a recipe, start by adding or subtracting 1 to 2 minutes. For example, if you're using large chicken breasts, you may need to add another minute to the cooking time, since we call for medium chicken breasts in our recipes. It's worth noting that if you have to stack your poultry or meat, it will not cook evenly and may take a little longer than we say, especially from frozen. We've said it once and we'll say it again: Cooking in the Instant Pot is part art and part science.

8. "What is Natural Release vs. Quick Release of pressure?"

When your meal is done cooking in the Instant Pot, the pressure that has built up inside the pot will have to be released before you can open the lid. Every recipe in our book will specify whether to allow the pressure to release naturally, quick release the pressure, or use a combination of the two. Here's the difference between them:

NATURAL RELEASE—When the cook time is through, you'll let the pressure release on its own until the float valve (sometimes called the "pin") drops. This usually takes 10 to 20 minutes. We use this technique for larger cuts of meat and egg casseroles to allow the food to finish cooking through gently.

QUICK RELEASE—When the cook time is through, you'll use the pressure release valve to immediately release all the pressure until the float valve drops. We use this method on recipes where the food could easily get overcooked, like chicken. If the release method doesn't affect the end result one way or another, we opt for this faster method.

In some recipes, we'll have you let the pressure release naturally for a specified time, then quick release the remaining pressure. Consult your manual to see where the pressure release valve is located and how to use it.

9. "I just opened my cooker to find that my meal isn't done! Now what?!"

Don't panic. We've been in your shoes many times. Perhaps your cut of meat is thicker than what we tested, or it got stacked in a weird way. Or, quite honestly, sometimes an Instant Pot has a mind of its own!

First of all, check to make sure the silicone ring inside the lid is fitted correctly. Then, make sure you have a good meat thermometer to help determine if any of the meat is undercooked (see our safe internal cooking temperatures chart on page 249). If you find your food isn't done, give it a stir, reseal, and cook at high pressure for 1 minute more, then quick release the pressure. Keep in mind that the time it takes to come to pressure is part of the additional cook time, so cook in additional 1- to 2-minute increments until the food is done to avoid overcooking. Say it with us now: "The Instant Pot is part art and part science!"

10. "Any tips so that I won't blow up my kitchen or totally ruin a recipe?"

Rest assured, this isn't your grandmother's pressure cooker. The Instant Pot is very safe if used correctly. Here are a few more tips to avoid any danger or recipe flops:

▸ *Don't overfill the pot.* Your pot will have a maximum fill line, so stick to that guide. Pressure cookers need headspace to build pressure, so don't fill them past that line.

▸ *Don't increase the cooking time when doubling a meal.* Usually it will require the same amount of time to cook, because a double batch will take longer to come to pressure.

▸ *Danger! Danger!* Never move the Instant Pot during the cooking process, whether it's building pressure, fully pressurized, or releasing pressure.

▸ *Back away when you release the pressure.* The steam will spray up in the air, so be sure to keep your face and hands (and any children!) out of the way.

▸ *After the pressure is released, open the lid away from you.* More hot steam will come out of the pot when you do this.

▸ *If your pot is very full of soup or sauce, sometimes it can splatter when the pressure is released.* If you're worried about that, just cover the spout loosely with a dish towel.

▸ *Start with an easy recipe that doesn't include an expensive cut of meat, like one of our chicken or vegetarian recipes.* That way you won't break the bank if you make a mistake.

11. (BONUS!) "Do I need to adjust the cook time for high altitude?"

Yep, you guys are just special, we guess. The general rule is to add 5 percent to your pressure cook time for every 1,000 feet above a 2,000 feet elevation. So, if you live at 5,000 feet and the recipe calls for a 20-minute cook time, you would increase it by 15 percent to 23 minutes. (Does your brain hurt yet?) The point is, if you're up high, you'll have to cook just a *little* longer.

freezer cooking basics

As you learn to harness the power of freezer cooking *and* slow cooking (or pressure cooking) through our guidance, you'll eat around the table more with those you love most, ease dinnertime stress, save money by not eating out as much, and consume healthy meals regularly. This way of cooking has been a win-win for us!

If you don't already have it, be sure to pick up our first cookbook, *From Freezer to Table*, where we walk you through everything you need to know about freezer cooking. It's a must-have resource to help you get dinner on the table night after night! While we elaborate much more in our previous book, here are five tips to get you started making delicious freezer meals.

5 STEPS FOR SUCCESSFUL FREEZER MEALS

1. Chill cooked dishes before freezing.

It's important to let freshly cooked dishes cool before placing them in the freezer. There are a number of reasons for this. First, putting still-warm foods in the freezer can raise the freezer's temperature. This can cause surrounding frozen items to partially thaw and refreeze, which can alter the taste and texture of those foods. Second, placing hot food in a plastic freezer bag or container can result in the plastic releasing chemicals into the food. Third, warm food freezes so slowly that ice crystals form on top, which can alter the texture of the freezer meal. To avoid bacteria contamination while allowing food to cool, never let perishable food sit out on the counter for longer than 2 hours.

2. Freeze in an airtight, freezer-safe container to avoid freezer burn.

Our preferred storage method for most of the recipes in this cookbook are BPA-free freezer bags. If prepping meals for the slow cooker, filled freezer bags can be placed flat in the freezer on a rimmed baking sheet to catch any drips and freeze the food quickly and in a space-saving shape. Remove the pan after the contents of the bags have frozen solid and then you can easily stack the meals. **If prepping meals for the Instant Pot, make sure to place the freezer bag into a circular container so it freezes in that shape** (see page 22). Make sure the circular container is smaller than the diameter of the Instant Pot to ensure the meal will easily fit into the pot later.

3. Freeze quickly and at the right temperature.

▸ *Store all foods at 0°F or lower to retain vitamin content, flavor, texture, and color.* Use a freezer thermometer to ensure this.

▸ *Do not crowd the freezer.* Leave enough room for air to circulate around the food, which helps it to freeze rapidly.

▸ *Never stack packages to be frozen.* Instead, spread them out in one layer on various shelves, stacking them only after they've frozen solid.

▸ *Store cooked foods (like soups) in small servings, when possible, to help them freeze quickly.* This also allows you to defrost only what you need.

4. Follow the recommended storage times for freezing meals.

From a safety standpoint, food that is properly packaged and safely frozen (kept at a constant temperature of 0°F or lower) can be frozen indefinitely. **However, our experience is that most freezer meals taste best when eaten within about 3 months,** but we have successfully used ones that were 6 to 9 months old. For more freezing time recommendations, consult the freezer storage chart in our first cookbook, *From Freezer to Table*.

5. Thaw frozen food properly.

That means no thawing perishable food on the counter or in the slow cooker! The good news is, there are four safe ways to defrost your food (see box, page 23).

COOKING FREEZER MEALS IN THE INSTANT POT

Prepping meals in bulk and cooking them from frozen in the Instant Pot is the ultimate time-saver. If you can master the art of Instant Pot freezer meals, your dinnertime hour will be revolutionized.

Here are a few tips and tricks to keep in mind when preparing and cooking a meal from frozen in the Instant Pot.

THE 8 DOS AND DON'TS OF FREEZER MEALS FOR THE INSTANT POT

1. DO split large cuts of meat into smaller portions.

Cutting large pieces of meat, like beef and pork roasts, into smaller portions before freezing results in a meal that cooks faster and more evenly.

2. DO adjust your spices.

Not only does freezing food increase the spice level a tad, but the Instant Pot does as well. If you have a sensitive palate, you may want to pull back on the spice.

3. DO NOT stack meat and poultry.

We've found that when cooking from frozen, meat (especially chicken!) will cook very unevenly if pieces are piled on top of one another. If the steam can't reach the food to cook it, the outside will get overcooked and the inside will still be raw.

Make every effort to place pieces of meat or poultry side by side when freezing, rather than on top of one another.

4. DO freeze your meal in a circular shape.

A handy way to do this is to place your ingredients in a large freezer bag and seal. Then, set the bag in the inner pot from your Instant Pot or another round container closely resembling that size/shape and put it in the freezer for a few hours. Once it's frozen, you can remove the pot or container.

5. DO sauté the meal before cooking.

We've found that sautéing the frozen meal in the Instant Pot for about 5 minutes releases some of the liquid and helps the pot come to pressure faster.

6. DO allow extra time for the pot to come to pressure.

When you put a frozen meal in the Instant Pot, it's going to take longer to come to pressure and start cooking than a fresh meal. The timing of this really depends on the volume of the food and the shape it was frozen in, but it will usually take the pot 20 to 30 minutes to come to pressure.

7. DO expect cooking times to vary.

You'll find in our cooking instructions that we give a time range when cooking in the Instant Pot from frozen (see our cooking times chart on page 251 for recommended times). This is because cooking times for frozen meals can vary. Start with the lower end of the suggested cooking time, then test the food's internal temperature. If it's not done, cook for a few more minutes.

8. DO NOT assume all freezer meals can be cooked from frozen.

We found that a few types of meals simply don't do as well from frozen. We'd hate for you to have a subpar result (especially if you're using an expensive cut of meat), so in a few instances, we'll instruct you to thaw your meal first.

4 SAFE WAYS TO DEFROST FROZEN MEALS

1. Thaw in the refrigerator.

The most effective and safest way to thaw a freezer meal is to put it in the refrigerator for 24 to 48 hours. The exact thawing time will depend on the size of the meal. Make sure to place it on a plate to catch any condensation or leaks. This method works best when you develop a meal plan at the beginning of the week and then move the freezer meals to the refrigerator a few days ahead of time. We realize that planning doesn't always happen a few days out, so there are two faster thawing methods you can use. As an aside, you may be surprised to learn that once you've safely thawed your raw or cooked frozen food in the refrigerator, you can still refreeze it if it's been stored at 40°F or lower. Just keep in mind that there may be a loss of quality due to the moisture lost through thawing and that you've used up some of its "fresh food" shelf life.

2. Thaw in cold water.

Another safe thawing option is to place the food in a leak-proof plastic bag and immerse it in cold water, changing the water every 30 minutes. This still takes a bit of time, but it's quicker than the refrigerator option. According to the USDA website, "Small packages of meat, poultry, or seafood—about a pound—may thaw in an hour or less. A 3- to 4-pound package may take 2 to 3 hours. For whole turkeys, estimate about 30 minutes per pound." After using this method of thawing, cook your food immediately.

3. Thaw in the microwave.

The fastest option is to microwave-defrost food in a microwave-safe dish, according to your microwave's instructions. This method is our least favorite because it tends to dry out and partially cook food. Regardless, sometimes you just need to quickly thaw something, so the microwave it is! Make sure to cook your food immediately after using this method.

4. Cook the frozen food in your Instant Pot.

This is one of the true advantages the Instant Pot has over the slow cooker. It can cook meals safely from frozen! If you've forgotten to thaw out a meal, just pop it in the Instant Pot, press a few buttons, and you're good to go! All our recipes include instructions for this. (See all our tips and tricks on page 20.)

COOKING SHORTCUTS

If we've learned anything about our readers, it's that you love a good shortcut. Keep a few of these ideas in your back pocket to make our easy recipes even easier.

Microwave your aromatics (i.e., onions, carrots, celery). When making a meal for the slow cooker, instead of pulling out your skillet to sauté veggies at the beginning of a recipe, you can microwave them instead. Simply toss them in a microwave-safe bowl with the oil called for in the recipe and then microwave until softened, usually about 5 minutes.

Use frozen prechopped veggies. You can almost always find these in your local grocery store.

Use your food processor to dice onions, carrots, and celery. Peel the veggies and coarsely chop them into large, evenly sized pieces. Toss them into your food processor and pulse a few times until they're diced, being cautious not to overprocess them.

Ask your butcher to trim roasts and ribs. Trimming cuts of meat can be time-consuming (and an icky mess!). We've found that most butchers are more than willing to trim meat for you if you ask them to.

Shred chicken in your stand mixer. Hate shredding cooked chicken as much as we do? Chop deboned cooked chicken into large chunks and toss them in the bowl of your stand mixer. Using the paddle attachment, mix on medium-low until the chicken is shredded to your desired texture.

Freeze leftover cooked rice or use store-bought precooked rice. Rice freezes nicely and can be used in recipes down the road. Just add a little liquid to it when thawing to keep it moist. You can also snag precooked rice (like Uncle Ben's brand) at the store if you don't have any in the freezer.

Make large batches of basic sauces, broth, and seasonings and freeze small portions to have on hand. You'll be patting yourself on the back when you pull out that fresh pesto or homemade marinara sauce in a pinch. Having a healthy stash of freezer staples can be a lifesaver! See chapter 6 to get started.

equipment

Before you begin, make sure you have the necessary tools to start stocking your freezer with healthy meals to make in your slow cooker or Instant Pot. These are some of our must-haves:

6-QUART SLOW COOKER WITH LID—We tested all the recipes in this book in the KitchenAid 6-quart slow cooker with standard lid, because it provides the most even low and high temperatures, according to outside research. Any decent 6-quart slow cooker will work, though.

6-QUART ELECTRIC PRESSURE COOKER— We tested every recipe in a 6-quart Instant Pot. See page 15 for what to look for when purchasing an electric pressure cooker and why we prefer the Instant Pot brand for our recipes.

GALLON-SIZE AND QUART-SIZE FREEZER BAGS—Look for BPA-free freezer (not storage) bags. We find these are the easiest to use for freezing the meals in this book.

DIGITAL MEAT THERMOMETER—This tool provides a trustworthy guide to doneness. A meat thermometer doesn't need to be pricey, just something that can quickly and accurately read the temperature.

WOODEN CUTTING BOARD—Since many of our recipes require you to remove the meat from the slow cooker or Instant Pot to be shredded or sliced, using a wooden cutting board ensures that chemicals from the plastic cutting boards don't leach into your food.

STAINLESS STEEL SLOTTED SPOON—In some recipes, you'll want to leave behind excess liquid when removing the cooked food from the cooker. We've found that using a stainless steel slotted spoon is the easiest way to do this. We don't recommend a plastic one since it may leach chemicals into your hot food.

STEAMER RACK/TRIVET (WITH HANDLES)—A handful of our Instant Pot recipes require this piece of equipment, which usually comes as an accessory with your pressure cooker. It can be used in a variety of ways.

POT HOLDERS—A set of pot holders, especially ones made specifically for use with the Instant Pot, make it much easier to lift the pot and steamer rack out of the cooker without burning yourself.

INSTANT POT SILICONE LID—Perfect to place on top of the steel pot to store a meal in the refrigerator before or after cooking.

1- TO 1½-QUART ROUND BAKING DISH OR 7-INCH ROUND PAN—This kind of dish, either glass or ceramic, will be used for making egg casseroles and French toast casseroles in the Instant Pot. It needs to be able to fit down inside your pot, so don't get one with handles.

In this section, you'll find easy, crowd-pleasing egg casseroles, French toast casseroles, and steel-cut oats recipes for both breakfast and brunch. The Instant Pot recipes work well for breakfast, but the slow cooker casseroles work best for brunch due to the cook time.

We know you want a slow cooker breakfast casserole that takes all night to cook and is waiting for you in the morning. However, we learned that 4 hours is the *perfect* cook time, and 8 hours will lead only to an overcooked, burned egg casserole. You can, however, cook these casseroles ahead of time, store them in the fridge, and rewarm individual servings in the microwave to serve for a quick breakfast. Our families also enjoy them as "breakfast for dinner."

If you're serving a crowd, the slow cooker recipe is the way to go for casseroles. That's because the Instant Pot recipe yield is cut in half due to space constraints. However, the advantage of the Instant Pot recipe is that it's easy to double the batch, make one now, and freeze the other to have on hand for a busy morning.

Brown Sugar and Cinnamon
Steel-Cut Oats, *page 42*

breakfast

5-INGREDIENT BREAKFAST CASSEROLE

With only five main ingredients, this recipe takes just minutes to prepare and is a satisfying start to the day for everyone, including your gluten-free eater. Feel free to add any favorite sautéed veggies or mix up the meat or cheese you use, or try its close cousin, the Denver Omelet Casserole (page 31).

Recipe Testing Team Tip: *"I placed it under the broiler in the oven for a few minutes to brown it up at the end. The result was really tasty for dinner, and it reheated well the next morning."* —Tanya P.

Slow Cooker • MAKES: 8 TO 10 SERVINGS

2 teaspoons avocado oil or olive oil

1 pound ground pork sausage or turkey sausage (or bacon, chopped)

Cooking spray

3 cups refrigerated or thawed* frozen shredded hash browns

2 cups shredded cheddar cheese

12 large eggs

1 cup milk

¼ teaspoon salt, plus more to taste

¼ teaspoon ground black pepper, plus more to taste

Optional toppings: hot sauce, salsa, ketchup

*It's really important that you thaw your frozen hash browns completely. (This usually takes overnight in the refrigerator.) Otherwise, you'll end up with a soggy casserole.

MAKE IT NOW

1   In a large skillet, heat the oil over medium-high heat until shimmery. Add the sausage and cook until browned and cooked through, breaking it up as it cooks. Drain any excess grease. *(Freezing instructions begin here.)*

2   Spray the slow cooker insert generously with cooking spray. Layer 1½ cups of the hash browns, half the sausage, and 1 cup of the cheese in the slow cooker, then repeat with the remaining hash browns, sausage, and cheese.

3   In a large bowl, whisk together the eggs, milk, salt, and pepper. Pour over the other ingredients in the slow cooker.

4   Cover and cook on Low for 4 hours, or until the center is set. Dab off any moisture from the top with a paper towel.

5   Taste and season with more salt and pepper. Serve warm, topped with hot sauce, salsa, or ketchup, if desired.

FREEZE FOR LATER: Follow step 1; let the sausage cool. In a large bowl, whisk together the eggs, milk, salt, and pepper. Pour the egg mixture into a gallon-size freezer bag or container and add the sausage, hash browns, and 1½ cups of the cheese. Seal tightly and freeze. Place the remaining ½ cup cheese in a small freezer bag or container. Seal and freeze alongside the egg mixture.

PREPARE FROM FROZEN: *Note: You may want to have salsa, hot sauce, or sour cream on hand.* Thaw. Spray the slow cooker with cooking spray. Transfer the egg mixture to the slow cooker and sprinkle the remaining ½ cup cheese over the top. Follow steps 4 and 5.

Instant Pot • MAKES: 4 OR 5 SERVINGS

Equipment Needed

Steamer rack/trivet with handles

1- to 1½-quart round baking dish or 7-inch round pan (with a flat bottom)

1 teaspoon avocado oil or olive oil

½ pound all-natural ground pork sausage or turkey sausage (or bacon, chopped)

Cooking spray

1½ cups refrigerated or thawed* frozen shredded hash browns

1 cup shredded cheddar cheese

6 large eggs

½ cup milk

¼ teaspoon salt, plus more to taste

⅛ teaspoon ground black pepper, plus more to taste

Optional toppings: hot sauce, salsa, ketchup

*It's really important that you thaw your frozen hash browns completely. (This usually takes overnight in the refrigerator.) Otherwise, you'll end up with a soggy casserole.

MAKE IT NOW

1   Set the 6-quart Instant Pot to "Sauté." Pour the oil into the pot and heat until shimmery. Add the sausage and cook until browned and cooked through, breaking it up as it cooks. Press "Cancel." Transfer the sausage to a paper towel–lined plate and set aside. Wipe out the remaining grease from the pot.

2   Generously spray a 1- to 1½-quart round baking dish or 7-inch round pan with cooking spray. Layer ¾ cup of the hash browns, half the sausage, and ½ cup of the cheese in the dish, then repeat with the remaining hash browns, sausage, and cheese.

3   In a large bowl, whisk together the eggs, milk, salt, and pepper. Pour over the ingredients in the dish. *(Freezing instructions begin here.)*

(CONTINUES)

4   Pour 1 cup water into the 6-quart Instant Pot. Place the baking dish on a steamer rack and lower it into the pot using the handles.

5   Lock and seal the lid. Cook at high pressure for 18 minutes, then let the pressure release naturally, about 10 minutes. Dab off any moisture from the top with a paper towel. (The casserole will look very moist, but it's done if it registers at least 160°F in the middle.) Wearing oven mitts, carefully remove the baking dish using the steamer rack handles.

6   Taste and season with more salt and pepper. Serve warm, topped with hot sauce, salsa, or ketchup, if desired.

FREEZE FOR LATER: Follow steps 1 through 3. Tightly wrap the baking dish in a few layers of plastic wrap and then a layer of foil, squeezing out as much excess air as possible. Freeze.

PREPARE FROM FROZEN: *Note: You may want to have hot sauce, salsa, or ketchup on hand.* Follow steps 4 and 5, but cook for 40 to 45 minutes. Then, follow step 6.

DENVER OMELET CASSEROLE

One of our family's recent summer vacations included a stop at an all-American diner featuring the biggest Denver omelet I've ever seen. Somehow I inhaled the whole thing! The combo of colorful peppers and onions, ham, and gooey cheddar cheese gets me every time. That's why we built on to the basic 5-Ingredient Breakfast Casserole (page 28) to give you this option for another easy breakfast or brunch. Feel free to add in some chopped mushrooms when you cook the peppers and onions to pack in even more traditional Denver omelet veggies.
—Rachel

Slow Cooker • **MAKES: 8 TO 10 SERVINGS**

1 to 2 tablespoons avocado oil or olive oil

½ yellow onion, diced

1 red bell pepper, diced

1 green bell pepper, diced

Pinch of red pepper flakes

Salt and ground black pepper

2 cups diced fully cooked ham (we recommend using ham steak)

Cooking spray

3 cups refrigerated or thawed* frozen shredded hash browns

2 cups shredded cheddar cheese

12 large eggs

1 cup milk

Optional toppings: salsa, hot sauce, sour cream

*It's really important that you thaw your frozen hash browns completely. (This usually takes overnight in the refrigerator.) Otherwise, you'll end up with a soggy casserole.

MAKE IT NOW

1   In a large skillet, heat the oil over medium-high heat until shimmery. Add the onion and bell peppers and cook, stirring, until they begin to soften, 4 to 5 minutes. Season lightly with the red pepper flakes, salt, and black pepper as they cook. After they are done, stir in the ham. *(Freezing instructions begin here.)*

2   Spray the slow cooker insert generously with cooking spray. Layer 1½ cups of the hash browns, half the veggie-ham mixture, and 1 cup of the cheese in the slow cooker, then repeat with the remaining hash browns, veggie-ham mixture, and cheese.

(CONTINUES)

3   In a large bowl, whisk together the eggs, milk, and ¼ teaspoon black pepper. Pour over the other ingredients in the slow cooker.

4   Cover and cook on Low for 4 hours, until the center is set. Dab off any moisture from the top with a paper towel.

5   Taste and season with more salt and black pepper. Serve warm, topped with salsa, hot sauce, or sour cream, if desired.

FREEZE FOR LATER: Follow step 1. In a large bowl, whisk together the eggs, milk, and ¼ teaspoon black pepper. Pour the egg mixture into a gallon-size freezer bag or container and add the ham-veggie mixture, hash browns, and 1½ cups of the cheese. Seal tightly and freeze. Place the remaining ½ cup cheese in a small freezer bag or container. Seal and freeze alongside the casserole.

PREPARE FROM FROZEN: *Note: You may want to have salsa, hot sauce, or sour cream on hand.* Thaw. Spray the slow cooker with cooking spray. Transfer the egg mixture to the slow cooker and sprinkle the remaining ½ cup cheese over the top. Follow steps 4 and 5.

Instant Pot • MAKES: 4 OR 5 SERVINGS

Equipment Needed
Steamer rack/trivet with handles

1- to 1½-quart round baking dish or 7-inch round pan (with a flat bottom)

1 teaspoon avocado oil or olive oil

¼ yellow onion, diced

½ red bell pepper, diced

½ green bell pepper, diced

Pinch of red pepper flakes

Salt and ground black pepper

1 cup diced fully cooked ham (we recommend ham steak)

Cooking spray

1½ cups refrigerated or thawed* frozen shredded hash browns

1 cup shredded cheddar cheese

6 large eggs

½ cup milk

Optional toppings: salsa, hot sauce, sour cream

*It's really important that you thaw your frozen hash browns completely. (This usually takes overnight in the refrigerator.) Otherwise, you'll end up with a soggy casserole.

(CONTINUES)

1   Set the 6-quart Instant Pot to "Sauté." Pour the oil into the pot and heat until shimmery. Add the onion and bell peppers and cook, stirring, until they begin to soften, 4 to 5 minutes. Season lightly with the red pepper flakes, salt, and pepper while they cook. After they are done, stir in the ham. Press "Cancel."

2   Generously spray a 1- to 1½-quart round baking dish or 7-inch round pan with cooking spray. Layer ¾ cup of the hash browns, half the veggie-ham mixture, and ½ cup of the cheese in the dish, then repeat with the remaining hash browns, veggie-ham mixture, and cheese.

3   In a medium bowl, whisk together the eggs, milk, and ⅛ teaspoon black pepper. Pour over the other ingredients in the baking dish. *(Freezing instructions begin here.)*

4   Pour 1 cup water into the Instant Pot. Place the baking dish on a steamer rack and lower it into the pot using the handles.

5   Lock and seal the lid. Cook at high pressure for 18 minutes, then let the pressure release naturally, about 10 minutes. Dab off any moisture from the top with a paper towel. (The casserole will look very moist, but it's done if it registers at least 160°F in the middle.) Wearing oven mitts, carefully remove the casserole using the steamer rack handles.

6   Taste and season with salt and black pepper. Serve warm, topped with salsa, hot sauce, or sour cream, if desired.

FREEZE FOR LATER: Follow steps 1 through 3. Tightly wrap the baking dish in a few layers of plastic wrap and then a layer of foil, squeezing out as much excess air as possible. Freeze.

PREPARE FROM FROZEN: *Note: You may want to have salsa, hot sauce, or sour cream on hand.* Follow steps 4 and 5, but cook for 40 to 45 minutes. Then, follow step 6.

BLUEBERRY FRENCH TOAST CASSEROLE WITH VANILLA GLAZE

Bonus points are given to this easy twist on French toast for a) making everybody happy, b) using up stale bread, and c) using less sugar than most versions.

Slow Cooker • **MAKES: 8 TO 10 SERVINGS**

8 large eggs

1 cup milk

4 tablespoons (½ stick) butter, melted

¼ cup pure maple syrup, plus more (optional) for serving

2 teaspoons pure vanilla extract

¼ teaspoon salt

Cooking spray

10 to 12 cups (1-inch cubes) stale or lightly toasted* sourdough, French, or whole-grain bread

2 cups fresh or frozen blueberries

Vanilla Glaze (recipe follows)

If you don't have stale bread on hand, preheat the oven to 350°F. Place your bread cubes on a rimmed baking sheet and bake for 10 to 15 minutes, stirring at least once, until toasted. Let the bread cool before using.

MAKE IT NOW

1   In a large bowl, whisk together the eggs, milk, melted butter, maple syrup, vanilla, and salt. (*Freezing instructions begin here.*)

2   Spray the slow cooker insert with cooking spray. Spread half the bread evenly over the bottom, then sprinkle half the blueberries evenly over the bread. Repeat with the remaining bread and blueberries. Pour the egg mixture evenly over the bread and blueberries. Make sure every piece of bread is moist. (At this point, you can cover and refrigerate for up to 24 hours.)

3   Cover and cook on Low for 4 hours, until the center is set. Let cool slightly.

4   Meanwhile, make the glaze. Use a spoon to drizzle the glaze over the casserole. Serve warm, with more maple syrup, if desired.

FREEZE FOR LATER: Follow step 1. Carefully place the bread, blueberries, and egg mixture in a gallon-size freezer bag or container. Seal, toss gently to combine, and freeze.

PREPARE FROM FROZEN: *Note: You will need to have the ingredients to make the Vanilla Glaze on hand.* Thaw. Spray the slow cooker with cooking spray. Transfer the bread mixture to the slow cooker. Follow steps 3 and 4.

(CONTINUES)

Equipment Needed

Steamer rack/trivet with handles

1- to 1½-quart round baking dish or 7-inch round pan (with a flat bottom)

Cooking spray

5 to 6 cups (1-inch cubes) stale or lightly toasted* sourdough, French, or whole-grain bread

1 cup fresh or frozen blueberries

4 large eggs

½ cup milk

2 tablespoons butter, melted

2 tablespoons pure maple syrup, plus more for serving

1 teaspoon pure vanilla extract

⅛ teaspoon salt

Vanilla Glaze (recipe follows)

*If you don't have stale bread on hand, preheat the oven to 350°F. Place your bread cubes on a rimmed baking sheet and bake for 10 to 15 minutes, stirring at least once, until toasted. Let the bread cool before using.

MAKE IT NOW

1   Generously spray a 1- to 1½-quart round baking dish or 7-inch round pan with cooking spray. Spread half the bread evenly over the bottom, then sprinkle half the blueberries evenly over the bread. Repeat.

2   In a medium bowl, whisk together the eggs, milk, butter, maple syrup, vanilla, and salt. Pour the egg mixture evenly over the bread and blueberries. Try to make sure every piece of bread is moist. *(Freezing instructions begin here.)* (At this point, you can cover the casserole and refrigerate for up to 24 hours.)

3   Pour 1 cup water into the 6-quart Instant Pot. Place the baking dish on a steamer rack and lower it into the pot using the handles.

4   Lock and seal the lid. Cook at high pressure for 15 minutes, then let the pressure release naturally, about 10 minutes. (The casserole is done when the center is set or registers 160°F.) Wearing oven mitts, carefully remove the baking dish using the steamer rack handles. Let cool slightly.

5   Meanwhile, make the glaze. Use a spoon to drizzle the glaze over the casserole. Serve warm, with more maple syrup, if desired.

FREEZE FOR LATER: Follow steps 1 and 2. Tightly wrap the uncooked casserole in a few layers of plastic wrap and then one or two layers of foil, squeezing out as much air as possible. Freeze.

PREPARE FROM FROZEN: *Note: You will need to have the ingredients to make the Vanilla Glaze and (optional) maple syrup on hand.* Follow steps 3 and 4, but cook the frozen casserole for 23 to 28 minutes. Then, follow step 5.

VANILLA GLAZE
MAKES: ¼ CUP

1 tablespoon milk

½ teaspoon pure vanilla extract

Pinch of salt

½ cup powdered sugar

In a small bowl, stir together the milk, vanilla, and salt. Add the powdered sugar and whisk until a thin, white glaze forms.

PUMPKIN PIE FRENCH TOAST CASSEROLE
WITH FRESH WHIPPED MAPLE CREAM

With vitamin A–rich pumpkin, protein-rich eggs and milk, and whole-grain bread, this baked French toast version of pumpkin pie is a nutritious way to start your day. To really give it that dessert-for-breakfast vibe, take one minute (literally) to whip up the decadent Fresh Whipped Maple Cream topping. Keep in mind that the texture of this casserole is more like bread pudding than a slice of French toast.

Slow Cooker • MAKES: 8 TO 10 SERVING

8 large eggs

1 cup milk

1 cup canned pumpkin puree (look for a BPA-free can)

½ cup pure maple syrup, plus more (optional) for serving

4 tablespoons (½ stick) butter, melted

2 teaspoons pure vanilla extract

2 teaspoons ground cinnamon

½ teaspoon ground nutmeg

½ teaspoon ground ginger

¼ teaspoon ground cloves

¼ teaspoon salt

Cooking spray

10 to 12 cups (1-inch cubes) stale or lightly toasted* sourdough, French, or whole-grain bread

Fresh Whipped Maple Cream (recipe follows)

Toasted pecans or candied pecans, coarsely chopped (optional)

*If you don't have stale bread on hand, preheat the oven to 350°F. Place your bread cubes on a rimmed baking sheet and bake for 10 to 15 minutes, stirring at least once, until toasted. Let cool before using.

MAKE IT NOW

1   In a large bowl, whisk together the eggs, milk, pumpkin, maple syrup, melted butter, vanilla, cinnamon, nutmeg, ginger, cloves, and salt. *(Freezing instructions begin here.)*

2   Spray the slow cooker insert generously with cooking spray. Spread all the bread over the bottom. Pour the egg mixture evenly over the bread. Try to make sure every piece of bread is moist. (At this point, you can cover the slow cooker insert and refrigerate for up to 24 hours.)

3   Cover and cook on Low for 4 hours, until the center is set.

(CONTINUES)

4   Just before serving, make the whipped cream.

5   Serve the casserole warm in bowls, topped with a dollop of the whipped cream and a sprinkling of toasted pecans or a little more maple syrup, if desired.

FREEZE FOR LATER: Follow step 1. Place the bread and the egg mixture in a gallon-size freezer bag or container. Seal, toss gently to combine, and freeze.

PREPARE FROM FROZEN: *Note: You will need to have the ingredients for the Fresh Whipped Maple Cream and maple syrup and nuts on hand.* Thaw. Spray the slow cooker with cooking spray. Transfer the bread-egg mixture to the slow cooker and follow steps 3 through 5.

Instant Pot • MAKES: 4 OR 5 SERVINGS

Equipment Needed

Steamer rack/trivet with handles

1- to 1½-quart round baking dish or 7-inch round pan (with a flat bottom)

4 large eggs

½ cup milk

½ cup canned pure pumpkin (look for a BPA-free can)

¼ cup pure maple syrup, plus more (optional) for serving

2 tablespoons butter, melted

1 teaspoon pure vanilla extract

1 teaspoon ground cinnamon

¼ teaspoon ground nutmeg

¼ teaspoon ground ginger

⅛ teaspoon ground cloves

⅛ teaspoon salt

Cooking spray

5 to 6 cups (1-inch cubes) stale or lightly toasted* sourdough, French, or whole-grain bread

Fresh Whipped Maple Cream (recipe follows)

Toasted pecans or candied pecans, coarsely chopped, for serving (optional)

*If you don't have stale bread on hand, preheat the oven to 350°F. Place your bread cubes on a rimmed baking sheet and bake for 10 to 15 minutes, stirring at least once, until toasted. Let cool before using.

MAKE IT NOW

1   In a large bowl, whisk together the eggs, milk, pumpkin, maple syrup, melted butter, vanilla, cinnamon, nutmeg, ginger, cloves, and salt.

2   Generously spray a 1- to 1½-quart round baking dish or 7-inch round pan with cooking spray. Spread all the bread over the bottom. Pour the egg mixture evenly over the bread. Try to make sure every piece of bread is moist. *(Freezing instructions begin here.)* (At this point, you can cover the baking dish and refrigerate for up to 24 hours.)

3   Pour 1 cup water into the 6-quart Instant Pot. Place the baking dish on a steamer rack and lower it into the pot using the handles.

4   Lock and seal the lid. Cook at high pressure for 15 minutes, then let the pressure release naturally, about 10 minutes. (The casserole is done when the center is set or registers 160°F.) Wearing oven mitts, carefully remove the baking dish using the steamer rack handles.

5   Just before serving, make the whipped cream.

6   Serve the casserole warm in bowls, topped with a dollop of the whipped cream and a sprinkling of toasted pecans or with a little more maple syrup, if desired.

FREEZE FOR LATER: Follow steps 1 and 2. Tightly wrap the uncooked casserole in a few layers of plastic wrap and then one or two layers of foil, squeezing out as much excess air as possible. Freeze.

PREPARE FROM FROZEN: *Note: You will need to have the ingredients for the Fresh Whipped Maple Cream and (optional) maple syrup and nuts on hand.* Follow steps 3 and 4, but cook for 23 to 28 minutes. Then, follow steps 5 and 6.

FRESH WHIPPED MAPLE CREAM
MAKES: 1½ TO 2 CUPS

| 1 cup cold heavy cream | 2 tablespoons pure maple syrup | ½ teaspoon pure vanilla extract |

In a chilled large metal bowl, combine the cream, maple syrup, and vanilla. Whisk with a hand mixer on high speed until it holds medium to stiff peaks, 30 to 60 seconds. Don't overmix the cream. The whipped cream can be covered and stored at the back of the refrigerator for up to 1 day.

BROWN SUGAR AND CINNAMON STEEL-CUT OATS

If you're looking for a no-fuss recipe that will wake you up in the morning with its delicious aroma, you've turned to the right page. Make sure to use steel-cut oats in this recipe. Regular oats will not hold up well if cooked in this way. Toasting the steel-cut oats at the get-go isn't a necessity, but it gives them a nutty flavor that sets them apart from other types of oats. Lastly, be sure to add milk to the finished product to get your desired consistency.

3 tablespoons butter (optional)

1½ cups steel-cut oats (gluten-free, if necessary)

Cooking spray (for slow cooker)

6 cups (for slow cooker) or 4½ cups (for Instant Pot) water or whole milk, plus more milk as needed

½ teaspoon salt

½ cup packed brown sugar

1 teaspoon ground cinnamon

Slow Cooker • MAKES: 6 SERVINGS

MAKE IT NOW

1 If you'd like to toast the oats, in a medium skillet, melt the butter over medium-high heat. Add the oats and cook, stirring often, for about 5 minutes, until fragrant.

2 Spray the slow cooker insert with cooking spray. Combine the oats, water or milk, salt, brown sugar, and cinnamon in the slow cooker and stir. Make sure all the oats are submerged in the liquid.

3 Cover and cook on Low for 6 to 8 hours. *(Freezing instructions begin here.)*

4 Stir in additional milk to reach the desired consistency. Serve warm.

FREEZE FOR LATER: Follow steps 1 through 3. Let the oatmeal cool, then divide it evenly among 6 greased jumbo muffin tins (or jumbo silicone muffin liners) to create single-serving portions. Freeze until frozen solid, then pop out the oatmeal portions and transfer them to a gallon-size freezer bag or container. Seal and freeze.

PREPARE FROM FROZEN: *Note: You will need milk to complete this meal.* Place a serving of frozen oatmeal in a microwave-safe bowl. Add about ⅓ cup milk and microwave in 30-second intervals, stirring between each, until warmed through. Add more milk as needed to reach the desired consistency.

Instant Pot • MAKES: 6 SERVINGS

MAKE IT NOW

1   If you'd like to toast the oats, set the 6-quart Instant Pot to "Sauté." Place the butter in the pot. When the butter has melted, add the oats and cook, stirring often, for about 5 minutes, until fragrant. Press "Cancel."

2   Add water or milk, salt, brown sugar, and cinnamon to the pot and stir. Make sure all the oats are submerged in the liquid.

3   Lock and seal the lid. Cook at high pressure for 12 minutes. Allow the pressure to release naturally for 10 minutes, then quick release the remaining pressure. When you open the pot, you'll notice there is excess liquid. Give it a stir to incorporate. *(Freezing instructions begin here.)*

4   Stir in additional milk to reach the desired consistency. Serve warm.

FREEZE FOR LATER: Follow steps 1 through 3. Let the oatmeal cool, then divide it evenly among 6 greased jumbo muffin tins (or jumbo silicone muffin liners) to create single-serving portions. Freeze until frozen solid, then pop out the oatmeal portions and transfer them to a gallon-size freezer bag or container. Seal and freeze.

PREPARE FROM FROZEN: *Note: You will need milk to complete this meal.* Place a serving of frozen oatmeal in a microwave-safe bowl. Add about ⅓ cup milk and microwave in 30-second intervals, stirring between each, until warmed through. Add more milk as needed to reach the desired consistency.

PEANUT BUTTER CUP STEEL-CUT OATS

High fives for a super-healthy steel-cut oats recipe that makes both kids and parents happy. The key to making this breakfast dish a win is how you serve it. Add a dollop of peanut butter and sprinkle some mini chocolate chips over the top. It feels like a tasty treat, and your body will thank you for this nutritional powerhouse meal. Filled with fiber, iron, and protein, it'll stick with you all morning long.

3 tablespoons butter (optional)

1½ cups steel-cut oats (look for gluten-free variety, if needed)

Cooking spray (for slow cooker)

6 cups (for slow cooker) or 4½ cups (for Instant Pot) water or whole milk, plus more milk as needed

3 tablespoons unsweetened cocoa powder

3 tablespoons pure maple syrup

1 teaspoon ground cinnamon

1 teaspoon pure vanilla extract

3 tablespoons all-natural peanut butter, plus more for serving

Mini chocolate chips and/or sliced bananas, for topping

Slow Cooker • **MAKES: 6 SERVINGS**

MAKE IT NOW

1   If you'd like to toast the oats, in a medium skillet, melt the butter over medium-high heat. Add the oats and cook, stirring often, for about 5 minutes, until fragrant.

2   Spray the slow cooker insert with cooking spray. Combine the oats, water or milk, cocoa powder, maple syrup, cinnamon, and vanilla in the slow cooker and stir until well combined.

3   Cover and cook on Low for 6 to 8 hours. Add the peanut butter and stir to combine. *(Freezing instructions begin here.)*

4   Stir in additional milk to reach the desired consistency. Serve topped with an additional scoop of peanut butter and some mini chocolate chips and/or sliced bananas.

FREEZE FOR LATER: Follow steps 1 through 3. Let the oatmeal cool, then divide it evenly among 6 greased jumbo muffin tins (or jumbo silicone muffin liners)

(CONTINUES)

to create single-serving portions. Freeze until frozen solid, then pop out the oatmeal portions and transfer them to a gallon-size freezer bag or container. Seal and freeze.

PREPARE FROM FROZEN: *Note: You will need milk, peanut butter, mini chocolate chips, and/or a banana to complete this meal.* Place a serving of frozen oatmeal in a microwave-safe bowl. Add about ⅓ cup milk and microwave in 30-second intervals, stirring between each, until warmed through. Follow step 4.

Instant Pot • MAKES: 6 SERVINGS

MAKE IT NOW

1   If you'd like to toast the oats, set the 6-quart Instant Pot to "Sauté." Place the butter in the pot. When the butter has melted, add the oats and cook, stirring often, for about 5 minutes, until fragrant. Press "Cancel."

2   Add the water or milk, cocoa powder, maple syrup, cinnamon, and vanilla to the pot and stir until well combined.

3   Lock and seal the lid. Cook at high pressure for 12 minutes. Allow the pressure to release naturally for 10 minutes, then quick release the remaining pressure. When you open the pot, you'll notice there is excess liquid. Give it a stir to incorporate. Add the peanut butter and stir to combine. *(Freezing instructions begin here.)*

4   Stir in additional milk to reach the desired consistency. Serve topped with an additional scoop of peanut butter and some mini chocolate chips and/or sliced bananas.

FREEZE FOR LATER: Follow steps 1 through 3. Let the oatmeal cool, then divide it evenly among 6 greased jumbo muffin tins (or jumbo silicone muffin liners) to create single-serving portions. Freeze until frozen solid, then pop out the oatmeal portions and transfer them to a gallon-size freezer bag or container. Seal and freeze.

PREPARE FROM FROZEN: *Note: You will need milk, peanut butter, mini chocolate chips, and/or a banana to complete this meal.* Place a serving of frozen oatmeal in a microwave-safe bowl. Add about ⅓ cup milk and microwave in 30-second intervals, stirring between each, until warmed through. Follow step 4.

APPLE MAPLE STEEL-CUT OATS

You can't beat a wholesome, fall-inspired breakfast. The beauty of this oatmeal is that you can easily adjust it at the end to your preferences. Add toasted pecans for a little crunch or additional maple syrup to sweeten it up to your heart's delight.

3 tablespoons butter (optional)

1½ cups steel-cut oats (gluten-free, if necessary)

Cooking spray (for slow cooker)

6 cups (for slow cooker) or 4½ cups (for Instant Pot) water or whole milk, plus more milk as needed

1 large apple, cored and diced

½ cup raisins

1 tablespoon ground cinnamon

⅓ cup pure maple syrup, plus more for serving

1 teaspoon pure vanilla extract

Slow Cooker • MAKES: 6 SERVINGS

MAKE IT NOW

1   If you'd like to toast the oats, in a medium skillet, melt the butter over medium-high heat. Add the oats and cook, stirring often, for about 5 minutes, until fragrant.

2   Spray the slow cooker insert with cooking spray. Combine the oats, water or milk, apple, raisins, cinnamon, maple syrup, and vanilla in the slow cooker and stir. Make sure all the oats are submerged in the liquid.

3   Cover and cook on Low for 6 to 8 hours. *(Freezing instructions begin here.)*

4   Stir in additional milk to reach the desired consistency. Serve warm.

FREEZE FOR LATER: Follow steps 1 through 3. Let the oatmeal cool, then divide it evenly among 6 greased jumbo muffin tins (or jumbo silicone muffin liners) to create single-serving portions. Freeze until frozen solid, then pop out the oatmeal portions and transfer them to a gallon-size freezer bag or container. Seal and freeze.

PREPARE FROM FROZEN: *Note: You will need milk to complete this meal.* Place a serving of frozen oatmeal in a microwave-safe bowl. Add about ⅓ cup milk and microwave in 30-second intervals, stirring between each, until warmed through. Add more milk as needed to reach the desired consistency.

(CONTINUES)

MAKE IT NOW

1   If you'd like to toast the oats, set the 6-quart Instant Pot to "Sauté." Place the butter in the pot. When the butter has melted, add the oats and cook, stirring often, for about 5 minutes. Press "Cancel."

2   Add the water or milk, apple, raisins, cinnamon, maple syrup, and vanilla to the pot and stir. Make sure all the oats are submerged in the liquid.

3   Lock and seal the lid. Cook at high pressure for 12 minutes. Allow the pressure to release naturally for 10 minutes, then quick release the remaining pressure. When you open the pot, you'll notice there is excess liquid. Give it a stir to incorporate. *(Freezing instructions begin here.)*

4   Stir in additional milk to reach the desired consistency. Serve warm.

FREEZE FOR LATER: Follow steps 1 through 3. Let the oatmeal cool, then divide it evenly among 6 greased jumbo muffin tins (or jumbo silicone muffin liners) to create single-serving portions. Freeze until frozen solid, then pop out the oatmeal portions and transfer them to a gallon-size freezer bag or container. Seal and freeze.

PREPARE FROM FROZEN: *Note: You will need milk to complete this meal.* Place a serving of frozen oatmeal in a microwave-safe bowl. Add about $\frac{1}{3}$ cup milk and microwave in 30-second intervals, stirring between each, until warmed through. Add more milk as needed to reach the desired consistency.

Garlic-Herb
Whole Chicken
with Gravy, *page 65*

chicken & turkey

CHEESY CHICKEN TAQUITOS

If you want a simple meal that goes directly from freezer to table in no time, this is it! Lean shredded chicken is turned into a creamy mixture with a hint of heat, then wrapped tightly in a tortilla and baked until crispy. So little work for such a great meal! Be sure to try the Shredded Beef and Cheese Taquitos (page 142), too.

1 to 1½ pounds boneless, skinless medium chicken breasts	1 cup low-sodium chicken broth, homemade (see page 240) or store-bought	1½ cups shredded cheddar cheese
2 tablespoons taco seasoning, homemade (see page 243) or store-bought	¼ cup cream cheese	Cooking spray
	¼ cup mild or medium salsa	*Optional toppings:* salsa, guacamole, sour cream or plain Greek yogurt
	8 (8-inch) whole-wheat tortillas	

Slow Cooker • MAKES: 4 SERVINGS (2 TAQUITOS PER SERVING)

MAKE IT NOW

1 Place the chicken in the slow cooker and rub the taco seasoning in on all sides. Add the broth.

2 Cover and cook on Low for 2½ to 3½ hours or until cooked through. (The chicken is done when it is no longer pink inside and/or registers 165°F internally.) Transfer the chicken to a cutting board. Pour ½ cup of the liquid from the slow cooker into a measuring cup and discard the rest. Using two forks, shred the chicken and return it to the slow cooker.

3 Add the cream cheese and salsa and stir until the cream cheese has melted. Add the reserved braising liquid, if the mixture looks dry. It should be creamy but not watery.

4 Arrange the tortillas on a flat surface. Top each tortilla with an equal amount of the chicken mixture, leaving a little room at the edges so the filling doesn't spill out. Top each with about 3 tablespoons of the cheddar. Roll up the tortillas very tightly. *(Freezing instructions begin here.)*

5 Preheat the oven to 400°F. Spray a rimmed baking sheet with cooking spray or line it with parchment paper.

(CONTINUES)

6   Arrange the taquitos tightly side by side on the baking sheet, seam-side down. Spray the tops with cooking spray and bake for 15 to 20 minutes, until the cheese has melted and the taquitos are golden brown.

7   Serve warm, with your favorite toppings.

FREEZE FOR LATER: Follow steps 1 through 4. Place the rolled taquitos seam-side down in even layers (separated with parchment paper, if needed) in a gallon-size freezer bag or container. Seal and freeze.

PREPARE FROM FROZEN: *Note: Have your favorite toppings on hand to complete this meal.* Two options:

1   Thaw. Follow steps 5 through 7.

2   Do not thaw. Follow steps 5 and 6, but cover the frozen taquitos with foil and bake for 25 minutes. Remove the foil and bake for 5 to 10 minutes more, until the taquitos are golden brown and completely warmed through. Follow step 7.

Instant Pot • MAKES: 4 SERVINGS (2 TAQUITOS PER SERVING)

MAKE IT NOW

1   Place the chicken in the 6-quart Instant Pot and rub in the taco seasoning on all sides. Add the broth.

2   Lock and seal the lid. Cook at high pressure for 7 minutes, then quick release the pressure. (The chicken is done when it is no longer pink inside and/or registers 165°F internally.) Transfer the chicken to a cutting board. Pour ½ cup of the liquid from the pot into a measuring cup and discard the rest. Using two forks, shred the chicken and return it to the pot.

3   Add the cream cheese and salsa and stir until the cream cheese has melted. Add the reserved braising liquid, if the mixture looks dry. It should be creamy but not watery.

4   Arrange the tortillas on a flat surface. Top each tortilla with an equal amount of the chicken mixture, leaving a little room at the edges so the filling doesn't spill out. Top each with about 3 tablespoons of the cheddar. Roll up the tortillas very tightly. *(Freezing instructions begin here.)*

5   Preheat the oven to 400°F. Spray a rimmed baking sheet with cooking spray or line it with parchment paper or foil.

6   Arrange the taquitos tightly side by side on the baking sheet, seam-side down. Spray the tops with cooking spray and bake for 15 to 20 minutes, until the cheese has melted and the taquitos are golden brown.

7   Serve warm, with your favorite toppings.

FREEZE FOR LATER: Follow steps 1 through 4. Place the rolled taquitos seam-side down in even layers (separated with parchment paper, if needed) in a gallon-size freezer bag or container. Seal and freeze.

PREPARE FROM FROZEN: *Note: Have your favorite toppings on hand to complete this meal.* Two options:

1   Thaw. Follow steps 5 through 7.

2   Do not thaw. Follow steps 5 and 6, but cover the frozen taquitos with foil and bake for 25 minutes. Remove the foil and bake for 5 to 10 minutes more, until the taquitos are golden brown and completely warmed through. Follow step 7.

ADELYN'S STICKY BBQ DRUMSTICKS

My daughter, Adelyn, *loves* drumsticks. They're her number one request if she gets to pick dinner. I feel like the flavor of this recipe is an accurate representation of her personality: sweet and just a little spicy. The secret to making these super-flavorful and crispy is using our Homemade BBQ Sauce (page 236) and then giving them a few minutes under the broiler at the end.

1½ tablespoons brown sugar

1½ teaspoons paprika

1½ teaspoons garlic powder

1½ teaspoons onion powder

1½ teaspoons salt

¾ teaspoon ground black pepper

2½ to 3 pounds bone-in, skin-on chicken drumsticks

1½ cups BBQ sauce, store-bought or homemade (see page 236), plus more for serving

---

Slow Cooker • MAKES: 4 TO 6 SERVINGS

MAKE IT NOW

1 In a small bowl, combine the brown sugar, paprika, garlic powder, onion powder, salt, and pepper. Sprinkle the seasoning evenly over the drumsticks and rub it in to coat all sides. *(Freezing instructions begin here.)*

2 Place the seasoned drumsticks in the slow cooker and cover with 1 cup of the BBQ sauce.

3 Cover and cook on Low for 3 to 4 hours or until cooked through. (The chicken is done when it registers 165°F internally.)

4 Position the top oven rack about 6 inches below the broiler. Preheat the broiler. Line a rimmed baking sheet with foil.

5 Use tongs to place the drumsticks on the prepared baking sheet; discard any liquid remaining in the slow cooker. Brush the chicken with ¼ cup of the BBQ sauce and broil until the chicken starts to brown and look crispy, 2 to 3 minutes. Flip the chicken over, brush with the remaining ¼ cup BBQ sauce, and broil until the skin begins to brown and look crispy, 2 to 3 minutes more.

6 Serve warm, with extra BBQ sauce for dipping.

(CONTINUES)

FREEZE FOR LATER: Follow step 1. Place the seasoned chicken and 1 cup of the BBQ sauce in a gallon-size freezer bag or container. Seal, toss to coat, and freeze. Pour the remaining 1/2 cup BBQ sauce into a small freezer bag or container. Seal and freeze alongside the chicken.

PREPARE FROM FROZEN: *Note: Have BBQ sauce on hand for serving.* Thaw. Transfer the chicken to the slow cooker and follow steps 3 through 6.

Instant Pot • MAKES: 4 TO 6 SERVINGS

MAKE IT NOW

1   In a small bowl, combine the brown sugar, paprika, garlic powder, onion powder, salt, and pepper. Sprinkle the seasoning evenly over the drumsticks and rub it in to coat all sides. *(Freezing instructions begin here.)*

2   Place the seasoned drumsticks in the 6-quart Instant Pot and cover with 1 cup of the BBQ sauce.

3   Lock and seal the lid. Cook at high pressure for 12 minutes, then quick release the pressure. (The chicken is done when it registers 165°F internally.)

4   Position the top oven rack about 6 inches below the broiler. Preheat the broiler. Line a rimmed baking sheet with foil.

5   Use tongs to place the drumsticks on the prepared baking sheet; discard any liquid remaining in the Instant Pot. Brush the chicken with 1/4 cup of the BBQ sauce and broil until the chicken starts to brown and look crispy, 2 to 3 minutes. Flip the chicken over, brush with the remaining 1/4 cup BBQ sauce, and broil until the skin begins to brown and look crispy, 2 to 3 minutes more.

6   Serve warm, with extra BBQ sauce for dipping.

FREEZE FOR LATER: Follow step 1. Place the chicken and 1 cup of the BBQ sauce in a gallon-size freezer bag or container (try not to stack the drumsticks in the bag/container as much as possible; instead, place them side by side). Seal, toss to coat, and freeze (if using a freezer bag, set it in a bowl or round container with a diameter similar to the Instant Pot so it will fit in the pot when frozen; see page 22). Pour the remaining 1/2 cup BBQ sauce into a small freezer bag or container. Seal and freeze alongside the chicken.

PREPARE FROM FROZEN: Thaw the BBQ sauce. Set the Instant Pot to "Sauté." Cook the frozen meal for about 5 minutes to release the liquid. Press "Cancel." Follow step 3, but cook for 17 to 22 minutes. Follow steps 4 through 6.

HONEY BOURBON CHICKEN

This sweet-and-spicy chicken dish takes minutes to throw together yet is complex in flavor, thanks to ingredients like fresh ginger, soy sauce, honey, and, of course, bourbon. The bourbon lends a smoky caramel-like sweetness that's hard to replicate. Don't worry, the alcohol will evaporate when the sauce is simmered at the end. Look for small bottles by the liquor counter. —Rachel

Recipe Testing Team Tip: *"I packed this for lunch in 24-ounce containers for the week and layered them with peas/rice/chicken/sauce. They were amazing all week long."* —Jamie

½ cup low-sodium soy sauce

⅓ cup honey

¼ cup organic or all-natural ketchup

¼ cup bourbon or other whiskey

2 tablespoons avocado oil or olive oil

1 tablespoon minced fresh ginger

4 garlic cloves, minced

¼ teaspoon red pepper flakes (decrease to ⅛ teaspoon, if sensitive to heat)

½ cup sliced green onions, plus more for garnish

1½ to 2 pounds boneless, skinless medium chicken breasts

2 tablespoons cornstarch

Cooked basmati rice or brown rice, for serving

Stir-fried vegetables, for serving (optional)

Slow Cooker • MAKES: 4 TO 6 SERVINGS

MAKE IT NOW

1 In a medium bowl, whisk together the soy sauce, honey, ketchup, bourbon, oil, ginger, garlic, red pepper flakes, and green onions. Add the chicken and stir to coat with the sauce. *(Freezing instructions begin here.)*

2 Place the chicken and sauce in the slow cooker. Cover and cook on Low for 2½ to 3½ hours or until cooked through. (The chicken is done when it is no longer pink inside and/or registers 165°F internally.) Carefully transfer the chicken to a wooden cutting board, dice or shred the meat, and set aside.

3 In a small bowl, stir together the cornstarch and 2 tablespoons water until smooth. Carefully pour the juices from the slow cooker into a medium saucepan. Add the cornstarch mixture and bring to a boil over high heat. Reduce the heat to maintain a simmer and cook, stirring, until the sauce has thickened, about 3 minutes.

(CONTINUES)

4   Return the chicken and sauce to the slow cooker. Stir gently to combine. Serve over basmati or brown rice. Garnish with green onions and serve with stir-fried vegetables, if desired.

FREEZE FOR LATER: Follow step 1. Pour the sauce and chicken into a gallon-size freezer bag or container. Seal and freeze.

PREPARE FROM FROZEN: *Note: Have cooked rice, cornstarch, and (optional) stir-fried veggies on hand to complete this meal.* Thaw. Follow steps 2 through 4.

Instant Pot • MAKES: 4 TO 6 SERVINGS

MAKE IT NOW

1   In the 6-quart Instant Pot, whisk together the soy sauce, honey, ketchup, bourbon, oil, ginger, garlic, red pepper flakes, and green onions. Add the chicken and stir to coat. *(Freezing instructions begin here.)*

2   Lock and seal the lid. Cook at high pressure for 7 minutes or until the chicken is cooked through, then quick release the pressure. (The chicken is done when it is no longer pink inside and/or registers 165°F internally.)

3   Transfer the chicken to a cutting board, dice or shred the meat, and set aside.

4   In a small bowl, stir together the cornstarch and 2 tablespoons water until smooth. Set the Instant Pot to "Sauté." Stir the cornstarch mixture into the sauce and bring to a boil. Cook, stirring, until the sauce has thickened, about 3 minutes. Press "Cancel."

5   Stir the chicken back into the sauce to combine. Serve over basmati or brown rice. Garnish with green onions and serve with stir-fried vegetables, if desired.

FREEZE FOR LATER: Follow step 1. Pour the sauce and chicken into a gallon-size freezer bag or container. Seal and freeze (if using a freezer bag, set it in a bowl or round container with a diameter similar to the Instant Pot so it will fit in the pot when frozen; see page 22).

PREPARE FROM FROZEN: *Note: Have cooked rice, cornstarch, and (optional) stir-fried veggies on hand to complete this meal.* Set the Instant Pot to "Sauté." Transfer the frozen meal to the pot and cook for 5 minutes to release some liquid. Press "Cancel." Follow step 2, but cook for 15 to 20 minutes, until the chicken is cooked through. Follow steps 3 through 5.

FIESTA LIME CHICKEN BOWLS

One recipe tester put it very well when she said, *"This* is the kind of freezer meal I live for. Drop and go, and tasty in the end!"* We couldn't agree more. These bowls were one of our testing team's favorites. The chicken becomes infused with the cilantro and lime flavors. When you experience all the Mexican-flavored chicken goodness over rice and topped with avocado, sour cream, and cheese, you'll probably wish you'd doubled the batch.

1½ pounds boneless, skinless medium chicken breasts

1 tablespoon taco seasoning, homemade (see page 243) or store-bought

2 cups mild salsa (or medium, if you want a little more heat)

¼ cup freshly squeezed lime juice (about 2 small limes)

⅓ cup chopped fresh cilantro (sub: chopped fresh parsley)

4 to 6 cups cooked brown rice

Optional toppings: diced avocado, sour cream or plain Greek yogurt*, shredded cheddar cheese*, salsa, lime wedges, chopped fresh cilantro, chopped tomatoes

*Omit if making dairy-free version

Slow Cooker • MAKES: 4 TO 6 SERVINGS

MAKE IT NOW

1   Season the chicken with the taco seasoning on all sides. *(Freezing instructions begin here.)*

2   Place the seasoned chicken, salsa, lime juice, and cilantro in the slow cooker and give it all a stir.

3   Cover and cook on Low for 2½ to 3½ hours or until cooked through. (The chicken is done when it is no longer pink inside and/or registers 165°F internally.)

4   Transfer the chicken to a cutting board and shred or dice it. Return the chicken to the juices in the slow cooker and stir to coat.

5   Serve the chicken with its cooking juices in a bowl over cooked rice with your favorite toppings.

FREEZE FOR LATER: Follow step 1. Place the seasoned chicken, salsa, lime juice, and cilantro in a gallon-size freezer bag or container. Seal and freeze. Place the cooked rice in a freezer bag or container. Seal and freeze alongside the chicken.

(CONTINUES)

PREPARE FROM FROZEN: *Note: Have your favorite toppings on hand to complete this meal.* Thaw. Place in the slow cooker. Follow steps 3 and 4. Reheat the rice in the microwave or over low heat on the stove, until warm. Stir in a little of the full-cooked cooking juices from the chicken to add moisture while it warms up. Follow step 5.

Instant Pot • MAKES: 4 TO 6 SERVINGS

MAKE IT NOW

1   Season the chicken with the taco seasoning on all sides. *(Freezing instructions begin here.)*

2   Place the seasoned chicken, salsa, lime juice, and cilantro in the 6-quart Instant Pot and give it all a stir.

3   Lock and seal the lid. Cook at high pressure for 7 minutes, then quick release the pressure. (The chicken is done when it is no longer pink inside and/or registers 165°F internally.)

4   Transfer the chicken to a cutting board and shred or dice it. Return the chicken to the juices in the pot and stir to coat.

5   Serve the chicken with its cooking juices in a bowl over cooked rice with your favorite toppings.

FREEZE FOR LATER: Follow step 1. Place the seasoned chicken, salsa, lime juice, and cilantro in a gallon-size freezer bag or round container (do not stack the chicken breasts in the bag/container; instead, place them side by side). Seal and freeze (if using a freezer bag, set it in a bowl or round container with a diameter similar to the Instant Pot so it will fit in the pot when frozen; see page 22). Place the cooked rice in a separate freezer bag or container. Seal and freeze alongside the chicken.

PREPARE FROM FROZEN: *Note: Have your favorite toppings on hand to complete this meal.* Set the rice on the counter to thaw. Set the Instant Pot to "Sauté." Transfer the frozen chicken to the pot and cook for 5 minutes to release some liquid. Press "Cancel." Follow step 2, but cook for 15 to 20 minutes. Reheat the rice in the microwave or over low heat on the stove, until warm. Stir in a little of the full-cooked cooking juices from the chicken to add moisture while it warms up. Follow steps 3 and 4.

GARLIC-HERB WHOLE CHICKEN
WITH GRAVY

This low-prep whole chicken turns out moist every single time. The fresh herbs, garlic, and onion hidden inside bring big flavor as they slowly marry with the chicken juices. These juices will be a key ingredient in the simple gravy that you'll serve over the finished product. Be sure to season the chicken liberally at the get-go, and don't skip the broiling step if you want a beautiful, crispy bird at the end. Serve with your favorite roasted veggies for a comforting, healthy meal you'll return to again and again.

Chicken

1 (4- to 5-pound) whole chicken

1 tablespoon butter, at room temperature, or olive oil

Salt and ground black pepper

5 sprigs fresh thyme

2 sprigs fresh rosemary

Handful of fresh parsley

½ head garlic, halved crosswise

½ onion, cut into 2-inch pieces

Gravy

2 tablespoons butter

2 tablespoons unbleached all-purpose flour

Salt and ground black pepper

Slow Cooker • **MAKES: 4 TO 6 SERVINGS**

MAKE IT NOW

1   *For the chicken:* If necessary, remove the neck and gizzards from the cavity of the chicken (save them to make chicken broth, if you'd like; see page 240). Pat the chicken dry and rub the butter all over the outside. Season the chicken generously inside and out with salt and pepper. Stuff the thyme, rosemary, parsley, garlic, and onion into the cavity. *(Freezing instructions begin here.)*

2   Place the chicken breast-side down in the slow cooker. Cover and cook on Low for 4 to 6 hours, until the chicken is cooked through. (The chicken is done when it registers 165°F near the inner thigh, between the leg and breast.)

3   Position the top oven rack about 8 inches below the broiler. Preheat the broiler.

4   Transfer the chicken to a baking dish, breast-side up. Broil for 3 to 4 minutes, until crispy and golden brown, keeping a close eye on the chicken so it doesn't burn. Tent with foil and let rest for about 20 minutes.

(CONTINUES)

5 *For the gravy:* While the chicken rests, in a medium saucepan, melt the butter over medium heat. Whisk in the flour and cook for 1 to 2 minutes, until the mixture becomes a smooth paste. Increase the heat to medium-high. While whisking, use a ladle or a dry measuring cup to slowly add the juices left in the slow cooker.* Whisk continuously until the gravy is smooth and thickened, 3 to 5 minutes. Taste and season with salt and pepper.

6 Carve the chicken. Serve warm, drizzled with the gravy.

To get super-smooth gravy, you may want to strain the juices before adding them to the pan.

FREEZE FOR LATER: Follow step 1. Place the chicken in a gallon-size freezer bag, if it will fit (have someone help you by holding the bag open), or wrap it tightly in a few layers of plastic wrap and then a few layers of foil. Freeze.

PREPARE FROM FROZEN: *Note: You will need to have butter, flour, salt, and pepper on hand to complete this meal.* Thaw. (It may take 2 to 3 days to thaw in the refrigerator.) Follow steps 2 through 6.

Instant Pot • MAKES: 4 TO 6 SERVINGS

Equipment Needed
Steamer rack/trivet with handles

MAKE IT NOW

1 *For the chicken:* If necessary, remove the neck and gizzards from the cavity of the chicken (save them to make chicken broth, if you'd like; see page 240). Pat the chicken dry and rub the butter all over the outside. Season the chicken generously inside and out with salt and pepper. Stuff the thyme, rosemary, parsley, garlic, and onion into the cavity. *(Freezing instructions begin here.)*

2 Pour 1 cup of water into the 6-quart Instant Pot. Place a steamer rack in the pot and set the chicken on it, breast-side down. Lock and seal the lid. Cook at high pressure for 24 to 30 minutes (6 minutes per pound, as a rule of thumb), then allow the pressure to release naturally, about 20 minutes. (The chicken is done when it registers 165°F near the inner thigh, between the leg and breast.)

3 Position the top oven rack about 8 inches below the broiler. Preheat the broiler.

4   Using pot holders, use the steamer rack to remove the chicken from the pot, then transfer it to a shallow baking dish, breast-side up. Broil for 3 to 4 minutes, until crispy and golden brown, keeping a close eye on the chicken so it doesn't burn. Tent with foil and let rest for about 20 minutes.

5   *For the gravy:* While the chicken rests, transfer the juices left in the pot to a glass measuring cup or a bowl. Set the Instant Pot to "Sauté." Place the butter in the pot. When the butter has melted, whisk in the flour and cook for 1 to 2 minutes, until the mixture becomes a smooth paste. While whisking, slowly pour in the juices and whisk continuously until the gravy is smooth and thickened, 3 to 5 minutes.* Taste and season with salt and pepper.

6   Carve the chicken. Serve warm, drizzled with the gravy.

To get super-smooth gravy, you may want to strain the juices before adding them to the pot.

FREEZE FOR LATER: Follow step 1. Place the chicken in a gallon-size freezer bag, if it will fit (have someone help you by holding the bag open), or wrap it tightly in a few layers of plastic wrap and then a few layers of foil. Freeze.

PREPARE FROM FROZEN: *Note: You will need to have butter, flour, salt, and pepper on hand to complete this meal.* Follow step 2, but cook the frozen chicken for 40 to 50 minutes (10 minutes per pound from frozen, as a rule of thumb). Follow steps 3 through 6.

GARLICKY CHICKEN THIGHS

Bone-in chicken thighs may not be your usual go-to cut of poultry, but they've won us over. That's because when cooked low and slow (or fast and at high pressure), bone-in thighs don't dry out easily. The mellow garlic, herb, and wine–infused sauce drizzled over this particular cut of meat provides a mouth-watering centerpiece to your meal. We suggest serving the chicken over rice, quinoa, or mashed potatoes with a side of steamed or roasted vegetables.

Shortcut: *Use pre-peeled garlic cloves from the refrigerated produce section of your grocery store.*

1 tablespoon avocado oil or olive oil	½ cup dry white wine (we suggest Chardonnay)	2 sprigs fresh thyme, or ½ teaspoon dried thyme
½ yellow onion, diced	½ cup low-sodium chicken broth, homemade (see page 240) or store-bought	3 bay leaves
Salt and ground black pepper		½ teaspoon celery salt
10 garlic cloves, peeled and left whole		3 pounds bone-in, skin-on chicken thighs

Slow Cooker • MAKES: 4 TO 6 SERVINGS

MAKE IT NOW

1   In a large skillet, heat the oil over medium-high heat until shimmery. Add the onion and cook, stirring frequently, until just slightly softened, 4 to 5 minutes, seasoning lightly with salt and pepper and stirring in the garlic during the last 30 to 60 seconds of cooking. Stir in the wine, broth, thyme, and bay leaves, scraping up any browned bits from the bottom of the pan. Remove from the heat.

2   In a small bowl, stir together 1½ teaspoons salt, ½ teaspoon pepper, and the celery salt. Pat dry the chicken thighs and season evenly with the spice mixture, rubbing it in on all sides. *(Freezing instructions begin here.)*

3   Place the chicken and onion-garlic sauce in the slow cooker. Cover and cook on Low for 3 to 4 hours or until cooked through. (The chicken is done when it registers 165°F internally.)

(CONTINUES)

4   Position the top oven rack about 6 inches below the broiler. Preheat the broiler. Line a baking dish with foil.

5   Using tongs, transfer the chicken thighs to the prepared baking dish and broil for 2 to 3 minutes, or until crispy and golden brown. Keep a close eye on it, so the chicken doesn't burn.

6   Discard the bay leaves and thyme sprigs from the sauce. Taste the sauce and season with salt and pepper.

7   To serve, spoon the sauce and garlic cloves over the chicken.

FREEZE FOR LATER: Follow steps 1 and 2. Let the onion-garlic sauce cool, then transfer it to a gallon-size freezer bag or container and add the seasoned chicken. Seal and freeze.

PREPARE FROM FROZEN: Thaw. Follow steps 3 through 7.

Instant Pot • MAKES: 4 TO 6 SERVINGS

MAKE IT NOW

1   Set the 6-quart Instant Pot to "Sauté." Pour the oil into the pot and heat until shimmery. Add the onion and cook, stirring frequently, until just slightly softened, 4 to 5 minutes, seasoning lightly with salt and pepper and stirring in the garlic during the last 30 to 60 seconds of cooking. Stir in the wine, broth, thyme, and bay leaves, scraping up any browned bits from the bottom of the pot. Press "Cancel."

2   In a small bowl, stir together 1½ teaspoons salt, ½ teaspoon pepper, and the celery salt. Pat dry the chicken thighs and season evenly with the spice mixture, rubbing it in on all sides. *(Freezing instructions begin here.)*

3   Nestle the chicken into the sauce in the Instant Pot.

4   Lock and seal the lid. Cook at high pressure for 12 minutes, then quick release the pressure. (The chicken is done when it registers 165°F internally.)

5   Position the top oven rack about 6 inches below the broiler. Preheat the broiler. Line a baking dish with foil.

6   Put the chicken thighs in the prepared baking dish and broil for 2 to 3 minutes, or until crispy and golden brown. Keep a close eye on it, so the chicken doesn't burn.

7   Discard the bay leaves and thyme sprigs from the sauce. Taste the sauce and season with salt and pepper.

8   To serve, spoon the sauce and garlic cloves over the chicken.

FREEZE FOR LATER: Follow steps 1 and 2. Let the onion-garlic sauce cool, then transfer it to a gallon-size freezer bag or round container and add the seasoned chicken (do not stack the chicken in the bag/container; instead, place the pieces side by side). Seal and freeze (if using a freezer bag, set it in a bowl or round container with a diameter similar to the Instant Pot so it will fit in the pot when frozen; see page 22).

PREPARE FROM FROZEN: Set the Instant Pot to "Sauté." Transfer the frozen meal to the pot and cook for 5 minutes to release some liquid. Press "Cancel." Follow step 4, but cook for 17 to 22 minutes. Follow steps 5 through 8.

CHICKEN PHILLY SUBS

Yep, just what it sounds like! Think classic Philly cheesesteak sub sandwiches but made with chicken. Since the flavors can get lost under the warm bread and cheese, we've ramped things up with some tangy pickled banana peppers and spicy pepper Jack cheese. Don't be afraid to drizzle a little of the juices from your cooker over the chicken right before broiling. You'll be glad you did!

Shortcuts: *If you don't mind the onions having a bit more crunch and stronger flavor to them, you can skip step 1 and make this a drop-and-go meal.*

1 tablespoon avocado oil or olive oil

1 large white or yellow onion, halved and thinly sliced into half-moons

2 garlic cloves, minced

2 green bell peppers, sliced

⅓ cup sliced jarred mild or hot banana peppers, drained

½ cup (for slow cooker) or 1 cup (for Instant Pot) low-sodium chicken broth, homemade (see page 240) or store-bought

1 teaspoon paprika

1 teaspoon salt

½ teaspoon ground black pepper

¼ teaspoon ground thyme

½ teaspoon cayenne pepper

½ teaspoon onion powder

¼ teaspoon red pepper flakes

1½ pounds boneless, skinless medium chicken breasts

6 whole-wheat hoagie rolls, split open three-quarters of the way

9 slices provolone or pepper Jack cheese

Slow Cooker • MAKES: 6 SANDWICHES

MAKE IT NOW

1   In a medium skillet, heat the oil over medium-high heat until shimmery. Add the onion and cook, stirring frequently, until just softened, about 4 minutes. Stir in the garlic during the last 30 to 60 seconds of cooking. *(Freezing instructions begin here.)*

2   Combine the onion-garlic mixture, bell peppers, banana peppers, and broth in the slow cooker and give everything a stir.

3   In a small bowl, stir together the paprika, salt, black pepper, thyme, cayenne, onion powder, and red pepper flakes. Season the chicken breasts evenly with the spice mixture, rubbing it in on all sides.

(CONTINUES)

4   Nestle the chicken in the slow cooker. Cover and cook on Low for 2½ to 3½ hours or until cooked through. (The chicken is done when it is no longer pink inside and/or registers 165°F internally.)

5   Transfer the chicken to a cutting board and slice it very thinly on an angle. Return the chicken to the slow cooker and stir it into the sauce to keep moist.

6   Position the top oven rack about 6 inches below the broiler. Preheat the broiler.

7   Place the rolls on a baking sheet with the insides facing up. Broil the rolls for 1 to 2 minutes, or until golden. Watch carefully so they do not burn.

8   Use a slotted spoon to place the chicken mixture inside the rolls. (Be sure to drain off as much liquid as possible as you do this.) Top each sandwich with 1½ slices of the cheese. Broil the open subs for 2 to 3 minutes more to melt the cheese before serving.

FREEZE FOR LATER: Follow step 1. Place the onion-garlic mixture, bell peppers, banana peppers, and broth in a gallon-size freezer bag or container. Follow step 3, then add the seasoned chicken to the same bag or container. Seal and freeze. Place the buns and cheese in separate freezer bags. Seal and freeze alongside the chicken.

PREPARE FROM FROZEN: Thaw. Follow steps 4 through 8.

Instant Pot • MAKES: 6 SANDWICHES

MAKE IT NOW

1   Set the 6-quart Instant Pot to "Sauté." Pour the oil into the pot and heat until shimmery. Add the onion and cook, stirring frequently, until just softened, about 4 minutes, stirring in the garlic during the last 30 to 60 seconds of cooking. Press "Cancel."

2   Add the bell peppers, banana peppers, and broth to the pot and give everything a stir.

3   In a small bowl, stir together the paprika, salt, black pepper, thyme, cayenne, onion powder, and red pepper flakes. Season the chicken breasts evenly with the spice mixture, rubbing it in on all sides. *(Freezing instructions begin here.)*

4   Nestle the chicken in the Instant Pot.

5   Lock and seal the lid. Cook at high pressure for 7 minutes, then quick release the pressure. (The chicken is done when it is no longer pink inside and/or registers 165°F internally.)

6   Transfer the chicken to a cutting board and slice it very thinly on an angle. Return it to the pot and stir it into the sauce to keep moist.

7   Position the top oven rack about 6 inches below the broiler. Preheat the broiler.

8   Place the rolls on a baking sheet with the insides facing up. Broil the rolls for 1 to 2 minutes, or until golden. Watch carefully so they do not burn.

9   Use a slotted spoon to place the chicken mixture inside the rolls. (Be sure to drain off as much liquid as possible as you do this.) Top each sandwich with 1½ slices of the cheese. Broil the open subs for 2 to 3 minutes more to melt the cheese before serving.

FREEZE FOR LATER: Follow steps 1 through 3. Place the seasoned chicken and the contents of the pot in a gallon-size freezer bag or round container (do not stack the chicken breasts in the bag/container; instead, place them side by side). Seal and freeze (if using a freezer bag, set it in a bowl or round container with a diameter similar to the Instant Pot so it will fit in the pot when frozen; see page 22). Place the buns and cheese in separate freezer bags. Seal and freeze alongside the chicken.

PREPARE FROM FROZEN: Thaw the buns and cheese. Set the Instant Pot to "Sauté." Transfer the frozen meal to the pot and cook for 5 minutes to release some liquid. Press "Cancel." Follow step 5, but cook for 15 to 20 minutes. Follow steps 6 through 9.

BAKED CHICKEN AND BLACK BEAN BURRITOS

Mexican ingredients make for some of our favorite slow cooker and Instant Pot recipes. This is probably why we have so many "south of the border"-style recipes in our cookbook! In this particular one, a veggie-packed chicken filling is made in your cooker of choice first. That filling is then wrapped up in tortillas, topped with cheese, and baked, resulting in a satisfying comfort meal that all ages enjoy.

1 to 2 tablespoons avocado oil or olive oil

1 onion, diced (about 1 cup)

1 green bell pepper, diced

1 red bell pepper, diced

2 garlic cloves, minced

1 (15-ounce) can black beans, drained and rinsed

1 cup medium salsa

2 tablespoons taco seasoning, homemade (see page 243) or store-bought

½ cup low-sodium chicken broth, homemade (see page 240) or store-bought (for Instant Pot only)

1½ pounds boneless, skinless medium chicken breasts

Cooking spray

8 (8-inch) whole-wheat tortillas

2 cups shredded cheddar cheese

Optional toppings: guacamole, sour cream or plain Greek yogurt, salsa

---

Slow Cooker • MAKES: 4 TO 6 SERVINGS (1 OR 2 BURRITOS PER SERVING)

MAKE IT NOW

1   In a large skillet, heat the oil over medium-high heat until shimmery. Add the onion and bell peppers and cook, stirring, until softened, 4 to 5 minutes. Stir in the garlic during the last 30 to 60 seconds of cooking.

2   Transfer the vegetables to the slow cooker. Add the beans, salsa, and taco seasoning to the slow cooker and stir to combine. Nestle the chicken into the mixture.

3   Cover and cook on Low for 2½ to 3½ hours or until cooked through. (The chicken is done when it is no longer pink inside and/or registers 165°F internally.)

4   Transfer the chicken to a cutting board and shred the meat with two forks. Return it to the slow cooker and stir.

5   Preheat the oven to 400°F (skip this if you'll be freezing the burritos to cook later). Grease a 9 × 13-inch baking dish with cooking spray.

6   Lay the tortillas out on a flat surface. Using a slotted spoon, spoon about ½ cup of the chicken-veggie mixture onto each tortilla (drain as much liquid as possible before placing on the tortilla). Add 2 tablespoons of the cheese to each tortilla. Roll them up and place them in the prepared baking dish, seam-side down, squeezing them in however they fit best. Top the burritos with the remaining 1 cup cheese. *(Freezing instructions begin here.)*

7   Bake for about 15 minutes, or until the cheese is melted and golden on top. Serve warm, with your favorite toppings.

FREEZE FOR LATER: Follow steps 1 through 6. Cover the baking dish with a lid or wrap tightly with a few layers of foil or plastic wrap and freeze.

PREPARE FROM FROZEN: *Note: Have your favorite toppings on hand to complete this meal.* Thaw. Preheat the oven to 400°F. Uncover the baking dish and follow step 7. (Alternatively, bake directly from frozen, covered in foil for 35–40 minutes and then uncovered for about 15 minutes.)

Instant Pot • **MAKES: 4 TO 6 SERVINGS (1 OR 2 BURRITOS PER SERVING)**

MAKE IT NOW

1   Set the 6-quart Instant Pot to "Sauté." Pour the oil into the pot and heat until shimmery. Add the onion and bell peppers and cook, stirring, until softened, 4 to 5 minutes. Stir in the garlic during the last 30 to 60 seconds of cooking. Press "Cancel."

2   Add the beans, salsa, taco seasoning, and broth to the pot and stir to combine. Nestle the chicken into the mixture.

3   Lock and seal the lid. Cook at high pressure for 7 minutes, then quick release the pressure. (The chicken is done when it is no longer pink inside and/or register 165°F internally.)

4   Transfer the chicken to a cutting board and shred the meat with two forks. Return it to the pot and stir.

5   Preheat the oven to 400°F (skip this if you'll be freezing the burritos to cook later). Grease a 9 × 13-inch baking dish with cooking spray.

(CONTINUES)

6   Lay the tortillas out on a flat surface. Using a slotted spoon, spoon about ½ cup of the chicken-veggie mixture onto each tortilla (drain as much liquid as possible before placing on the tortilla). Add 2 tablespoons of the cheese to each tortilla. Roll them up and place them in the prepared baking dish, seam-side down, squeezing them in however they fit best. Top the burritos with the remaining 1 cup cheese. *(Freezing instructions begin here.)*

7   Bake for about 15 minutes, or until the cheese is melted and golden on top. Serve warm, with your favorite toppings.

FREEZE FOR LATER: Follow steps 1 through 6. Cover the baking dish with a lid or wrap tightly with a few layers of foil or plastic wrap and freeze.

PREPARE FROM FROZEN: *Note: Have your favorite toppings to complete this meal.* Thaw. Preheat the oven to 400°F. Uncover the baking dish and follow step 7. (Alternatively, bake directly from frozen, covered in foil for 35–40 minutes and then uncovered for about 15 minutes.)

SOUTHWEST CHICKEN AND BACON WRAPS

We first had wraps similar to these many years ago at Flat Branch Pub & Brewing, one of our local hot spots in town, and we were hooked! This slow cooker version is our re-creation of that restaurant fave, and the result is now a regular weeknight recipe for our families. If you have some extra time, marinate the chicken about an hour before cooking for a boost of flavor. You can always play with the cheeses by subbing in Pepper Jack or a Mexican cheese blend.

Shortcut: *For the Creamy Southwest Ranch Sauce, you can mix equal parts salsa and store-bought ranch dressing. Look for an organic or all-natural version of each.*

¾ cup low-sodium chicken broth, homemade (see page 240) or store-bought

2 tablespoons cider vinegar

2 tablespoons freshly squeezed lime or lemon juice

2 garlic cloves, minced

1 tablespoon chopped fresh cilantro or parsley, or 1 teaspoon dried parsley

1 teaspoon chili powder

1 teaspoon ground cumin

½ teaspoon dried oregano

1 teaspoon salt

½ teaspoon ground black pepper

1½ pounds boneless, skinless medium chicken breasts

6 (8-inch) whole-wheat tortillas (or use gluten-free wraps, if preferred)

6 slices bacon, cooked and crumbled

1 cup shredded Colby Jack or cheddar cheese

Shredded lettuce, for serving

Chopped tomatoes, for serving

Creamy Southwest Ranch Sauce (recipe follows)

Slow Cooker • **MAKES: 6 WRAPS**

MAKE IT NOW

1   In a small bowl, whisk together the broth, vinegar, lime juice, garlic, cilantro, chili powder, cumin, oregano, salt, and pepper. *(Freezing instructions begin here.)*

2   Place the chicken in the slow cooker and pour the marinade over the top. If time allows, cover the slow cooker insert and place in the fridge to marinate the chicken for an hour or so.

(CONTINUES)

3   Cover and cook on Low for 2½ to 3½ hours or until cooked through. (The chicken is done when it is no longer pink inside and/or registers 165°F internally.)

4   Transfer the chicken to a cutting board and dice it.

5   Arrange the tortillas on a flat surface. To serve, top each tortilla with some chicken, bacon, cheese, lettuce, tomatoes, and Creamy Southwest Ranch Sauce, then fold over the sides of the tortilla to form a wrap.

FREEZE FOR LATER: Follow step 1. Place the chicken in a gallon-size freezer bag or container and pour in the marinade. Seal and freeze. Place the tortillas, bacon, and cheese in separate small freezer bags or containers. Seal and freeze next to the chicken.

PREPARE FROM FROZEN: *Note: You will need to have lettuce, tomatoes, and Creamy Southwest Ranch Sauce on hand to complete this meal.* Thaw. Transfer the chicken and marinade to the slow cooker and follow steps 3 through 5.

Instant Pot • MAKES: 6 WRAPS

MAKE IT NOW

1   In a small bowl, whisk together the broth, vinegar, lime juice, garlic, cilantro, chili powder, cumin, oregano, salt, and pepper. *(Freezing instructions begin here.)*

2   Place the chicken in the 6-quart Instant Pot and pour the marinade over the top. If time allows, cover the pot and marinate the chicken in the fridge for an hour or so.

3   Lock and seal the lid. Cook at high pressure for 7 minutes or until the chicken is cooked through, then quick release the pressure. (The chicken is done when it is no longer pink inside and/or registers 165°F internally.)

4   Transfer the chicken to a cutting board and dice it.

5   Arrange the tortillas on a flat surface. To serve, top each tortilla with some chicken, bacon, cheese, lettuce, tomatoes, and Creamy Southwest Ranch Sauce, then fold over the sides of the tortilla to form a wrap.

(CONTINUES)

FREEZE FOR LATER: Follow step 1. Place the chicken in a gallon-size freezer bag or container and pour in the marinade (do not stack the chicken breasts in the bag/container; instead, place them side by side). Seal and freeze (if using a freezer bag, set it in a bowl or round container with a diameter similar to the Instant Pot so it will fit in the pot when frozen; see page 22). Place the tortillas, bacon, and cheese in separate small freezer bags or containers. Seal and freeze next to the chicken.

PREPARE FROM FROZEN: *Note: You will need to have lettuce, tomatoes, and Creamy Southwest Ranch Sauce on hand to complete this meal.* Thaw the tortillas, bacon, and cheese. Set the Instant Pot to "Sauté." Transfer the frozen meal to the pot and cook for 5 minutes to release some liquid. Press "Cancel." Follow step 3, but cook for 15 to 20 minutes. Follow steps 4 and 5.

CREAMY SOUTHWEST RANCH SAUCE

MAKES: ABOUT 1 CUP

½ cup salsa

½ cup sour cream

1 tablespoon freshly squeezed lime or lemon juice

1 tablespoon minced fresh cilantro or parsley, or 1 teaspoon dried parsley

¼ teaspoon salt

¼ teaspoon ground black pepper

¼ teaspoon garlic powder

¼ teaspoon onion powder

Pinch of cayenne pepper

In a small bowl, stir together all the ingredients until combined. Cover and refrigerate for up to 1 week. Do not freeze.

JACK'S CHICKEN-AND-DUMPLING STEW

One of the best parts of creating recipes for our cookbooks and blog is involving my kids in the process. My son, Jack, decided that we had to have a chicken-and-dumplings recipe in this book. My entire family lapped these up for dinner and asked for leftovers in their lunch boxes the next day. The slow cooker and Instant Pot both produce a perfectly cooked, moist dumpling within minutes. I'm never going back to the stovetop for this total comfort meal. —Rachel

Stew

1 to 2 tablespoons butter

1 medium yellow onion, diced (about 1 cup)

2 celery stalks, sliced ¼ inch thick

4 carrots, sliced ¼ inch thick (about 1½ cups)

Salt and ground black pepper

1 teaspoon poultry seasoning

3 garlic cloves, minced

1½ to 2 pounds boneless, skinless chicken thighs, trimmed

4 cups low-sodium chicken broth, homemade (see page 240) or store-bought

2 bay leaves

1 cup frozen peas

Dumplings

1½ cups unbleached all-purpose flour

2 teaspoons baking powder

½ teaspoon salt

¾ teaspoon sugar

1½ teaspoons dried parsley

4 tablespoons (½ stick) butter

¾ cup milk

Slow Cooker • MAKES: 6 SERVINGS

MAKE IT NOW

1 *For the stew:* In a large skillet, melt the butter over medium-high heat. Add the onion, celery, and carrots and cook, stirring, until they just begin to soften, 4 to 5 minutes, seasoning lightly with salt and pepper and stirring in the poultry seasoning and garlic during the last 30 to 60 seconds of cooking. Remove from the heat. *(Freezing instructions begin here.)*

2 Transfer the vegetables to the slow cooker. Lightly season both sides of the chicken with salt and pepper and place in the slow cooker. Add the broth and bay leaves and stir to combine.

3 Cover and cook on Low for 3 to 4 hours. (The chicken is done when it registers 165°F internally.) Transfer the chicken to a cutting board and set

(CONTINUES)

aside. Remove and discard the bay leaves (make sure to return the lid to the cooker quickly). Set the slow cooker to High.

4   *For the dumplings:* In a medium bowl, whisk together the flour, baking powder, salt, sugar, and parsley. In a small microwave-safe bowl, microwave the butter and milk together until warm, about 1 minute, then whisk to melt the butter and combine. Stir the wet mixture into the dry mixture until just combined (do not overmix).

5   Working quickly and using a soup spoon or tablespoon, uncover the slow cooker, scoop out heaping tablespoons of dumpling batter, and drop into the stew. Try to spread the dumplings out so they cover the whole surface. Replace the lid quickly. Cook on High for 30 to 40 minutes or until the dumplings have doubled in size and a toothpick inserted into the center of a dumpling comes out clean.

6   Meanwhile, shred or chop the chicken into bite-size pieces and set aside.

7   When the dumplings are done, gently stir the chicken and peas into the stew. Taste and season with salt and pepper as needed. Serve.

FREEZE FOR LATER: Follow step 1. Let the veggies cool. Season both sides of the chicken lightly with salt and pepper and place the chicken in a gallon-size freezer bag or container. Add the broth, bay leaves, and cooled veggies. Seal and freeze. Combine the flour, baking powder, salt, sugar, and parsley in a quart-size freezer bag or container. Seal and freeze alongside the stew.

PREPARE FROM FROZEN: *Note: You will need to have butter, milk, and frozen peas on hand to complete this meal.* Thaw. Transfer the chicken-vegetable mixture to the slow cooker and follow steps 3 through 7, using the bag of dry mix to make the dumplings in step 4.

Instant Pot • MAKES: 6 SERVINGS

MAKE IT NOW

1   *For the stew:* Set the 6-quart Instant Pot to "Sauté." Place the butter in the pot. When the butter has melted, add the onion, celery, and carrots and cook, stirring, until they just begin to soften, 4 to 5 minutes, seasoning lightly with salt and pepper and stirring in the poultry seasoning and garlic during the last 30 to 60 seconds of cooking. Press "Cancel." *(Freezing instructions begin here.)*

(CONTINUES)

2   Season both sides of the chicken with salt and pepper. Add the chicken, broth, and bay leaves to the pot and stir to combine.

3   Lock and seal the lid. Cook at high pressure for 6 minutes, then quick release the pressure. (The chicken is done when it registers 165°F internally.) Transfer the chicken to a cutting board and set aside. Remove and discard the bay leaves.

4   *For the dumplings:* In a medium bowl, whisk together the flour, baking powder, salt, sugar, and parsley. In a small microwave-safe bowl, microwave the butter and milk together until warm, about 1 minute, then whisk to melt the butter and combine. Stir the wet mixture into the dry mixture until just combined (do not overmix).

5   Set the 6-quart Instant Pot to "Sauté" and bring the stew to a boil. Using a soup spoon or tablespoon, scoop out heaping tablespoons of dumpling batter, and drop into the stew. (Wet your hands to prevent sticking and use them to help slide the batter off the spoon and into the stew.) Try to spread the dumplings out so they cover the whole surface and aren't on top of one another. Cover the Instant Pot loosely with the lid, leaving a crack. Cook for about 12 minutes, until the dumplings double in size and a toothpick inserted into the center of a dumpling comes out clean. Press "Cancel."

6   Meanwhile, shred or chop the chicken into bite-size pieces and set aside.

7   When the dumplings are done, gently stir the chicken and peas into the stew. Taste and season with salt and pepper as needed. Serve.

FREEZE FOR LATER: Follow step 1. Let the veggies cool. Season both sides of the chicken lightly with salt and pepper and place the chicken in a gallon-size freezer bag or round container (do not stack the chicken thighs in the bag/container; instead, place them side by side). Add the broth, bay leaves, and cooled veggies. Seal and freeze (if using a freezer bag, set it in a bowl or round container with a diameter similar to the Instant Pot so it will fit in the pot when frozen; see page 22). Combine the flour, baking powder, salt, sugar, and parsley in a quart-size freezer bag or container. Seal and freeze alongside the stew.

PREPARE FROM FROZEN: *Note: You will need to have butter, milk, and frozen peas on hand to complete this meal.* Set aside the dry dumpling mix. Set the Instant Pot to "Sauté." Transfer the frozen stew to the pot and cook for 5 minutes to release some liquid. Press "Cancel." Follow step 3, but cook at high pressure for 15 to 20 minutes. Follow steps 4 through 7, using the bag of dry mix to make the dumplings in step 4.

ASIAN TURKEY MEATBALLS
WITH SWEET SOY DIPPING SAUCE

While we do occasionally like some authentic Asian takeout, we *love* making Asian-inspired food at home. The fresh flavors seem to stand out more, and recipes like these turkey meatballs come together quickly. Browning the meatballs at the beginning helps them hold their shape. Now, the key to making these meatballs *awesome* is the sweet soy dipping sauce. You simply can't skip it. Serve these over a bed of rice with some steamed vegetables and you'll have yourself a pretty darn healthy meal!

Meatballs

1 to 1¼ pounds lean ground turkey

¼ cup finely chopped green onions (about 3)

¼ cup finely chopped fresh cilantro or fresh parsley (about ½ bunch)

2 garlic cloves, minced

1 tablespoon sesame oil

2 tablespoons low-sodium soy sauce

¾ cup whole-wheat panko bread crumbs

1 large egg, beaten

1 to 2 tablespoons avocado oil or olive oil (for Instant Pot only)

Dipping Sauce

½ cup low-sodium soy sauce

½ cup honey

3 tablespoons unseasoned rice vinegar

1 tablespoon sesame oil

2 green onions, sliced

1½ tablespoons grated fresh ginger

Pinch of red pepper flakes

Cooked brown rice, for serving (optional)

Slow Cooker • MAKES: 4 SERVINGS

MAKE IT NOW

1   *For the meatballs:* Line a rimmed baking sheet with foil. In a large bowl, combine the turkey, green onions, cilantro, garlic, sesame oil, soy sauce, bread crumbs, and egg. Mix well using your hands. Shape the turkey mixture into roughly 1½-inch-diameter (tablespoon-size) meatballs and place them on the prepared baking sheet. *(Freezing instructions begin here.)*

(CONTINUES)

2   Position the top oven rack about 6 inches below the broiler. Preheat the broiler. Broil the meatballs for 4 to 5 minutes, until they are browned on the outside and some fat is rendered. (They will not be cooked through yet.)

3   *For the dipping sauce:* In the slow cooker, stir together the soy sauce, honey, vinegar, oil, onions, ginger, and pepper flakes.

4   Transfer the meatballs to the slow cooker. Cover and cook on Low for 2 to 3 hours. (The meatballs are done when they register at least 165°F internally.)

5   Serve with the dipping sauce from the slow cooker on the side, or over brown rice, with the dipping sauce drizzled over the top.

FREEZE FOR LATER: Follow step 1. Place the raw meatballs (do *not* broil the meatballs before freezing them, as it is not safe to freeze partially cooked meat) in even layers in a gallon-size freezer bag or container, being careful not to smash them; use parchment paper to separate the layers, if needed. Seal and freeze flat. Add all the dipping sauce ingredients into a quart-size freezer bag or container. Seal, shake to combine, and freeze alongside the meatballs.

PREPARE FROM FROZEN: *Note: You may want to have (optional) cooked brown rice on hand for serving.* Thaw. Follow step 2. Transfer the dipping sauce to the slow cooker, then follow steps 4 and 5.

Instant Pot • MAKES: 4 SERVINGS

Equipment Needed

Steamer rack/trivet with handles

MAKE IT NOW

1   *For the meatballs:* In a large bowl, combine the turkey, green onions, cilantro, garlic, sesame oil, soy sauce, bread crumbs, and egg. Mix well using your hands. Shape the turkey mixture into roughly 1½-inch-diameter (tablespoon-size) meatballs and place them on a plate. *(Freezing instructions begin here.)*

(CONTINUES)

2   Set the 6-quart Instant Pot to "Sauté." Pour the oil into the pot and heat until shimmery. Working in batches, brown the meatballs on all sides, 5 minutes or so. (Meatballs will not be cooked through yet.) Press "Cancel." Transfer the browned meatballs to a paper towel–lined plate (you can use the one from before) and wipe out any grease from the pot.

3   *For the dipping sauce:* In the pot, stir together the soy sauce, honey, vinegar, oil, onions, ginger, and pepper flakes.

4   Place the trivet in the pot (this prevents the meatballs from scorching on the bottom). Arrange the browned meatballs in one layer on the trivet. They will fit in there tightly.

5   Lock and seal the lid. Cook at high pressure for 5 minutes, then quick release the pressure. (The meatballs are done when they register 165°F internally.)

6   Serve the meatballs with the dipping sauce from the pot on the side, or over brown rice with the dipping sauce drizzled over the top.

FREEZE FOR LATER: Follow step 1. Place the raw meatballs (do *not* brown the meatballs before freezing them, as it is not safe to freeze partially cooked meat) in even layers in a gallon-size freezer bag or container, being careful not to smash them; use parchment paper to separate the layers, if needed. Seal and freeze flat. Add all the dipping sauce ingredients into a quart-size freezer bag or container. Seal, shake to combine, and freeze alongside the meatballs.

PREPARE FROM FROZEN*: *Note: You may want to have (optional) cooked brown rice on hand for serving.* Set the Instant Pot to "Sauté." Transfer the frozen dipping sauce to the pot and cook for 2 to 3 minutes to thaw the sauce. Follow steps 4 through 6. (The frozen meatballs will cook in the same amount of time as fresh ones.)

Meatballs cooked directly from frozen won't have as firm a texture because the browning step has been skipped. Feel free to thaw them first and brown them as directed in step 2, if you have time.

HAWAIIAN CHICKEN

Chicken, pineapple, red peppers, and onions cook in a sweet, sticky sauce with a hint of heat in the background. The chunks of pineapple and red peppers make for a colorful, pretty dish when served over rice.

¼ cup honey

¼ cup soy sauce

2 tablespoons dark brown sugar

1 tablespoon minced or grated fresh ginger

2 garlic cloves, minced

Pinch of red pepper flakes

½ cup low-sodium chicken broth, homemade (see page 240) or store-bought (for Instant Pot only)

1 tablespoon avocado oil or olive oil

1 yellow onion, cut into 1-inch chunks

1½ to 2 pounds boneless, skinless medium chicken breasts

2 cups (1-inch chunks) fresh pineapple or drained canned pineapple chunks

1 large or 2 small red bell peppers, chopped into 1-inch pieces

2 tablespoons cornstarch

Cooked basmati rice or brown rice, for serving

Slow Cooker • **MAKES: 4 TO 6 SERVINGS**

MAKE IT NOW

1   In a medium bowl, whisk together the honey, soy sauce, brown sugar, ginger, garlic, red pepper flakes, and broth. Set aside.

2   In a medium skillet, heat the oil over medium-high heat. Add the onion and cook, stirring, until just softened, 4 to 5 minutes. *(Freezing instructions begin here.)*

3   Transfer the onion to the slow cooker and add the chicken, pineapple, and bell peppers. Pour the honey sauce over the top.

4   Cover and cook on Low for 2½ to 3½ hours or until cooked through. (The chicken is done when it is no longer pink inside and/or registers 165°F internally.)

5   Transfer the chicken to a cutting board and slice it on an angle. Set aside.

6   Carefully transfer the veggies and juices from the slow cooker to a medium saucepan. In a small bowl, stir together the cornstarch and 2 tablespoons water until smooth, then add it to the pan with the veggies. Bring the mixture to a boil over high heat. Reduce the heat to maintain a simmer and cook, whisking, until thickened, about 3 minutes.

(CONTINUES)

7   Return chicken, thickened sauce, and veggies to the slow cooker and stir gently to combine. Serve over rice.

FREEZE FOR LATER: Follow steps 1 and 2; let the onion cool. Transfer the sauce and onion to a gallon-size freezer bag or container and add the chicken, pineapple, and bell peppers. Seal and freeze.

PREPARE FROM FROZEN: *Note: Have cornstarch and cooked rice on hand to complete this meal.* Thaw. Place in the slow cooker. Follow steps 4 through 7.

Instant Pot • MAKES: 4 TO 6 SERVINGS

MAKE IT NOW

1   In a medium bowl, whisk together the honey, soy sauce, brown sugar, ginger, garlic, red pepper flakes, and broth. Set aside.

2   Set the 6-quart Instant Pot to "Sauté." Pour the oil into the pot and heat until shimmery. Add the onion and cook, stirring, until just softened, 4 to 5 minutes. Press "Cancel." *(Freezing instructions begin here.)*

3   Add the chicken, pineapple, and bell peppers. Pour the honey sauce on top.

4   Lock and seal the lid. Cook at high pressure for 7 minutes or until the chicken is cooked through, then quick release the pressure.

5   Transfer the chicken to a cutting board and slice it on an angle. Set aside.

6   Set the Instant Pot to "Sauté." In a small bowl, stir together the cornstarch and 2 tablespoons water until smooth. Stir the cornstarch mixture into the veggies and sauce in the pot and bring to a boil. Cook, whisking, until thickened, about 3 minutes. Press "Cancel."

7   Return the chicken to the pot and stir gently to combine. Serve over rice.

FREEZE FOR LATER: Follow steps 1 and 2. Transfer the sauce and onion to a gallon-size freezer bag or container and add the chicken, pineapple, and bell peppers. Seal and freeze.

PREPARE FROM FROZEN: *Note: You will need to have cornstarch and rice on hand to complete this meal.* Set the Instant Pot to "Sauté." Transfer the frozen meal to the pot and cook for 5 minutes to release some liquid. Press "Cancel." Follow step 4, but cook for 15 to 20 minutes. Follow steps 5 through 7.

ULTIMATE CHICKEN AND BACON SANDWICHES

Create the ultimate chicken sandwiches for any weeknight by prepping and freezing all the components ahead of time. This well-seasoned, versatile shredded chicken also works to top a salad or in a wrap. If you're using your Instant Pot, cook the bacon in the pot first to save on dishes. Rachel loves to stir some BBQ sauce into the shredded chicken at the end. Polly prefers them without it. Either way, it's a delicious win!

¼ cup olive oil

¼ cup cider vinegar

2 teaspoons garlic powder

1½ teaspoons salt

1 teaspoon ground black pepper

1 teaspoon ground ginger

1 teaspoon paprika

1 teaspoon onion powder

1½ pounds boneless, skinless medium chicken breasts

1 cup low-sodium chicken broth, homemade (see page 240) or store-bought (for Instant Pot only)

4 whole-wheat hamburger buns

4 slices cheddar cheese

6 slices uncured bacon, cooked and broken in half

Optional toppings: lettuce, tomato slices, mayonnaise, BBQ sauce (see page 236), etc.

Slow Cooker • MAKES: 4 SANDWICHES

MAKE IT NOW

1   Place the oil, vinegar, garlic powder, salt, pepper, ginger, paprika, and onion powder in a gallon-size freezer bag or container. Seal and shake to combine. Add the chicken to the marinade, seal, and toss to coat. *(Freezing instructions begin here.)*

2   Marinate the chicken in the refrigerator for at least 2 hours and up to 24 hours.

3   Transfer the chicken and the marinade to the slow cooker. Cover and cook on Low for 2½ to 3½ hours or until cooked through. (The chicken is done when it is no longer pink inside and/or registers 165°F internally.)

4   Transfer the chicken to a wooden cutting board and shred or dice the meat. Return the chicken to the cooker to keep it warm and moist.

5   Position the top oven rack about 6 inches below the broiler. Preheat the broiler.

6   Place the buns on a baking sheet with the insides facing up. Broil the buns for about 1 minute, until golden brown. (Watch closely so they don't burn.)

7   Using a slotted spoon, top each bun with some of the chicken. For the ultimate sandwich, top each with a slice of cheese, 3 half pieces of bacon, and your favorite toppings. Serve.

FREEZE FOR LATER: Follow step 1. Freeze the chicken in the marinade. Place the buns, cheese, and bacon in separate freezer bags or containers. Seal and freeze alongside the chicken.

PREPARE FROM FROZEN: *Note: Have your favorite toppings on hand to complete this meal.* Thaw. Follow steps 3 through 7.

Instant Pot • MAKES: 4 SANDWICHES

MAKE IT NOW

1   Place the oil, vinegar, garlic powder, salt, pepper, ginger, paprika, and onion powder in a gallon-size freezer bag or container. Seal and shake to combine. Add the chicken to the marinade, seal, and toss to coat. *(Freezing instructions begin here.)*

2   Marinate the chicken in the refrigerator for at least 2 hours and up to 24 hours.

3   Transfer the chicken and the marinade to the 6-quart Instant Pot and add the broth. Lock and seal the lid. Cook at high pressure for 7 minutes, then quick release the pressure. (The chicken is done when it is no longer pink inside and/or registers 165°F internally.)

4   Transfer the chicken to a wooden cutting board and shred or dice the meat. Return the chicken to the pot to keep it warm and moist.

5   Position the top oven rack about 6 inches below the broiler. Preheat the broiler.

6   Place the buns on a baking sheet with the insides facing up. Broil the buns for about 1 minute, until golden brown. (Watch closely so they don't burn.)

7   Using a slotted spoon, top each bun with some of the chicken. For the ultimate sandwich, top each with a slice of cheese, 3 half pieces of bacon, and your favorite toppings. Serve.

FREEZE FOR LATER: Follow step 1. Make sure the chicken breasts aren't stacked in the bag/container; instead, place them side by side. Reseal, if necessary, and freeze (if using a freezer bag, set it in a bowl or round container with a diameter

(CONTINUES)

similar to the Instant Pot so it will fit in the pot when frozen; see page 22). Place the buns, cheese, and bacon in separate freezer bags or containers. Seal and freeze alongside the chicken.

PREPARE FROM FROZEN: *Note: You will need to have broth and your favorite toppings on hand to complete this meal.* Follow step 3, but cook the chicken for 15 to 20 minutes. Follow steps 4 through 7.

PESTO CHICKEN SAMMIES

These cute little sammies make a great appetizer—especially for a wedding or baby shower—or a light lunch or dinner. Whole chicken produces a super-moist end result and is an economical choice. Pesto stirred in at the end of this recipe adds big fresh flavor, and the feta lends a tangy, salty bite.

1 (4- to 5-pound) whole chicken	Salt and ground black pepper	½ cup (4 ounces) crumbled feta cheese
1 tablespoon avocado oil or olive oil	1 to 1½ cups pesto, homemade (see page 239) or refrigerated (not jarred) store-bought	12 mini whole-wheat buns or rolls, sliced in half

---

Slow Cooker • MAKES: 6 SERVINGS AS AN ENTRÉE OR 12 AS AN APPETIZER

MAKE IT NOW

1   If necessary, remove the neck and gizzards from the cavity of the chicken (save them to make chicken broth, if you'd like; see page 240). Pat the chicken dry and rub the oil all over the outside. Season the chicken generously inside and out with salt and pepper. *(Freezing instructions begin here.)*

2   Place the chicken breast-side down in the slow cooker. Cover and cook on Low for 4 to 6 hours, until the chicken is cooked through. (The chicken is done when it registers 165°F near the inner thigh, between the leg and breast.)

3   Using tongs or two spatulas, carefully transfer the chicken to a cutting board. Once it's cool enough to handle, shred the meat and place it in a medium bowl.

4   Add the pesto and feta to the shredded chicken and gently toss to combine. Serve warm or cold on the mini buns.

FREEZE FOR LATER: Follow step 1. Place the chicken in a gallon-size freezer bag, if it will fit (have someone help you by holding the bag open), or wrap it tightly in a few layers of plastic wrap and then a few layers of foil. Freeze. Place the pesto, feta, and buns in separate freezer bags or containers. Seal and freeze alongside the chicken.

PREPARE FROM FROZEN: Thaw. Follow steps 2 through 4.

(CONTINUES)

Instant Pot • MAKES: 6 SERVINGS AS AN ENTRÉE OR 12 AS AN APPETIZER

Equipment Needed
Steamer rack/trivet with handles

MAKE IT NOW

1   If necessary, remove the neck and gizzards from the inner cavity of the chicken (save them to make chicken broth, if you'd like; see page 240). Pat the chicken dry and rub the oil all over the outside. Season the chicken generously inside and out with salt and pepper. *(Freezing instructions begin here.)*

2   Pour 1 cup water into the 6-quart Instant Pot. Place the steamer rack in the pot and set the chicken on it, breast-side down. Lock and seal the lid. Cook at high pressure for 24 to 30 minutes (6 minutes per pound, as a rule of thumb), then allow the pressure to release naturally, about 20 minutes. (The chicken is done when it registers 165°F near the inner thigh, between the leg and breast.)

3   Using pot holders, use the steamer rack to remove the chicken from the pot, then transfer it to a cutting board. Once it's cool enough to handle, shred the meat and place it in a medium bowl.

4   Add the pesto and feta to the shredded chicken and gently toss to combine. Serve warm or cold on the mini buns.

FREEZE FOR LATER: Follow step 1. Place the chicken in a gallon-size freezer bag, if it will fit (have someone help you by holding the bag open), or wrap it tightly in a few layers of plastic wrap and then a few layers of foil. Freeze. Place the pesto, feta, and buns in separate freezer bags or containers. Seal and freeze alongside the chicken.

PREPARE FROM FROZEN: Thaw the pesto, feta, and buns. Follow step 2, but cook the frozen chicken for 40 to 50 minutes (10 minutes per pound, as a rule of thumb). Follow steps 3 and 4.

TERIYAKI CHICKEN THIGHS

This is a dream recipe for big-batch cooking. It doesn't require a lot of ingredients, there is no precooking before assembly, and the main ingredient, chicken thighs, is easy on the budget. The extra step of thickening the sauce at the end gives this recipe that signature glossy teriyaki sauce that will coat every bite.

½ cup low-sodium soy sauce

½ cup finely diced onion (about ½ onion)

2 garlic cloves, minced

¼ cup unseasoned rice vinegar

2 tablespoons brown sugar

¼ cup honey

1½ to 2 pounds boneless, skinless chicken thighs, trimmed

2 tablespoons cornstarch

Cooked rice (your favorite type), for serving

Sliced green onions, for garnish

Stir-fried veggies, for serving (optional)

Slow Cooker • MAKES: 4 TO 6 SERVINGS

MAKE IT NOW

1   In a medium bowl, combine the soy sauce, onion, garlic, vinegar, brown sugar, and honey. Add the chicken and toss to coat. *(Freezing instructions begin here.)*

2   Transfer the chicken and marinade to the slow cooker. Cover and cook on Low for 3 to 4 hours. (The chicken is done when it registers 165°F internally.)

3   Transfer the chicken from the slow cooker to a cutting board and shred the meat. Set aside.

4   Carefully pour or ladle the juices from the slow cooker into a medium saucepan. In a small bowl, stir together the cornstarch and 2 tablespoons water until smooth, then add the cornstarch mixture to the pan with the juices and bring to a boil over high heat. Reduce the heat to maintain a simmer and cook, stirring, until thickened, about 3 minutes.

5   Return the chicken and thickened sauce to the slow cooker. Stir gently to combine.

6   Serve over a bed of rice, garnished with green onions. Serve with stir-fried vegetables, if desired.

FREEZE FOR LATER: Follow step 1. Place the chicken and marinade in a gallon-size freezer bag or container. Seal and freeze.

PREPARE FROM FROZEN: *Note: You will need to have cornstarch, rice, green onions, and stir-fried veggies (optional) on hand to complete this meal.* Thaw. Follow steps 2 through 6.

Instant Pot • MAKES: 4 TO 6 SERVINGS

MAKE IT NOW

1   In a medium bowl, combine the soy sauce, onion, garlic, vinegar, brown sugar, and honey. Add the chicken and toss to coat. *(Freezing instructions begin here.)*

2   Transfer the chicken and marinade to the 6-quart Instant Pot.

3   Lock and seal the lid. Cook at high pressure for 7 minutes, then quick release the pressure.

4   Transfer the chicken to a cutting board and shred the meat. Set aside.

5   Set the Instant Pot to "Sauté." In a small bowl, stir together the cornstarch and 2 tablespoons water until smooth. Stir the cornstarch mixture into the sauce and bring to a boil. Cook, stirring, until it begins to thicken, about 3 minutes. Press "Cancel."

6   Return the chicken to the pot and stir gently to combine.

7   Serve over a bed of rice, garnished with green onions. Serve with stir-fried vegetables, if desired.

FREEZE FOR LATER: Follow step 1. Place the chicken and marinade in a gallon-size freezer bag or round container (do not stack the chicken thighs in the bag/container; instead, place them side by side). Seal and freeze (if using a freezer bag, set it in a bowl or round container with a diameter similar to the Instant Pot so it will fit in the pot when frozen; see page 22).

PREPARE FROM FROZEN: *Note: You will need cornstarch, rice, green onions, and stir-fried veggies (optional) to complete this meal.* Set the Instant Pot to "Sauté." Transfer the frozen meal to the pot and cook for 5 minutes to release some liquid. Press "Cancel." Follow step 3, but cook for 15 to 20 minutes. Follow steps 4 through 7.

ASIAN LETTUCE WRAPS

We love that this dish is low-carb and filled with lean meat and vegetables, but also seasoned well with amazing Asian staples like soy sauce, fresh ginger, sesame oil, and more. These wraps work well as an appetizer or for a lighter dinner. Beware! They can be messy, so have napkins on hand. Kid-friendly tip: Wrap the rice and chicken-veggie mixture in a whole-grain tortilla.

6 tablespoons low-sodium soy sauce

3 tablespoons unseasoned rice vinegar

3 tablespoons honey

1½ tablespoons sesame oil

1 teaspoon hot chile sauce (or up to 2 teaspoons if you prefer more heat), plus more (optional) for serving

3 garlic cloves, minced

1 tablespoon minced fresh ginger

1 teaspoon avocado oil or peanut oil

1 pound ground chicken or ground turkey

2 cups shredded coleslaw mix, or 1 cup shredded carrots and 1 cup shredded cabbage, plus more for garnish

1 bunch green onions, chopped

1 (8-ounce) can water chestnuts, drained and chopped

16 crisp Boston, Bibb, butter, or romaine lettuce leaves

½ cup peanuts, crushed

Slow Cooker • MAKES: 4 SERVINGS (2 OR 3 LETTUCE WRAPS PER SERVING)

MAKE IT NOW

1   In a small bowl, whisk together the soy sauce, vinegar, honey, sesame oil, chile sauce, garlic, and ginger. Set aside.

2   In a medium skillet, heat the oil over medium-high heat until shimmery. Add the ground chicken and cook until there is no more pink. Drain off any grease. (*Freezing instructions begin here.*)

3   Transfer the chicken to the slow cooker and add the coleslaw mix, green onions, and water chestnuts. Pour the sauce over the top and stir to combine.

4   Cover and cook on Low for 3 to 4 hours, until the vegetables are soft and the flavors have combined.

5   Set the lettuce leaves cupped-side up on a large plate or platter. Using a slotted spoon, fill each leaf with the chicken mixture. Top with more coleslaw mix, the crushed peanuts, and more chile sauce, if you like. Wrap the filling in the lettuce and eat it like a taco.

(CONTINUES)

FREEZE FOR LATER: Follow steps 1 and 2. Let the chicken cool. Place the chicken, sauce, coleslaw mix, green onions, and water chestnuts in a gallon-size freezer bag or container. Seal and freeze. Place the crushed peanuts in a small freezer bag or container. Seal and freeze alongside the chicken.

PREPARE FROM FROZEN: *Have lettuce leaves and coleslaw mix and (optional) chile sauce on hand to finish this meal.* Thaw. Follow steps 3 through 5.

Instant Pot • MAKES: 4 SERVINGS (2 OR 3 LETTUCE WRAPS PER SERVING)

MAKE IT NOW

1   In a small bowl, whisk together the soy sauce, vinegar, honey, sesame oil, chile sauce, garlic, and ginger. Set aside.

2   Set the 6-quart Instant Pot to "Sauté." Pour the oil into the pot and heat until shimmery. Add the ground chicken and cook until there is no more pink, breaking it up with a wooden spoon as it cooks. Drain off any grease. Press "Cancel."

3   Add the coleslaw mix, green onions, and water chestnuts. Pour the sauce over the top and stir to combine. (*Freezing instructions begin here.*)

4   Lock and seal the lid. Cook at high pressure for 5 minutes, then quick release the pressure.

5   Set the lettuce leaves cupped-side up on a large plate or platter. Using a slotted spoon, fill each leaf with the chicken mixture. Top with more coleslaw mix, the crushed peanuts, and more chile sauce, if you like. Wrap the filling in the lettuce and eat it like a taco.

FREEZE FOR LATER: Follow steps 1 through 3. Transfer the chicken mixture to a gallon-size freezer bag or round container. Seal and freeze (if using a freezer bag, set it in a bowl or round container with a diameter similar to the Instant Pot so it will fit in the pot when frozen; see page 22). Place the crushed peanuts in a small freezer bag or container. Seal and freeze alongside the chicken.

PREPARE FROM FROZEN: *Note: You will need to have lettuce leaves, coleslaw mix, and (optional) hot chile sauce on hand to finish this meal.* Set the peanuts on the counter to thaw. Set the Instant Pot to "Sauté." Transfer the frozen chicken mixture to the pot and cook for 5 minutes to release some liquid. Press "Cancel." Follow step 4, but cook for 10 to 15 minutes. Follow step 5.

CILANTRO-LIME CHICKEN NACHOS

When my husband is out of town and I need an easy meal that I know the kids will like, this is my go-to recipe. Not only does it come together fast, but it can be customized to each person's preference. "Tyler, here's your corner of the pan without beans. Adelyn, extra tomatoes? Be my guest! Clay, you want only cheese? Sure. Not fighting battles tonight." Load these nachos with as many veggies or toppings as you want and enjoy! —Polly

½ cup packed fresh cilantro, chopped

¾ cup salsa

Juice of 2 limes (about ¼ cup)

4 garlic cloves, minced

2 tablespoons ground cumin

2 teaspoons salt

1 teaspoon red pepper flakes

3 pounds boneless, skinless medium chicken breasts

1 (13-ounce) bag tortilla chips

4 cups shredded cheddar cheese

Optional toppings: diced avocado, salsa, chopped tomatoes, chopped fresh cilantro, black beans, sour cream, shredded lettuce, etc.

Slow Cooker • MAKES: 8 SERVINGS

MAKE IT NOW

1   In a small bowl, whisk together the cilantro, salsa, lime juice, garlic, cumin, salt, and red pepper flakes. *(Freezing instructions begin here.)*

2   Place the chicken in the slow cooker and pour the sauce over the top.

3   Cover and cook on Low for 2½ to 3½ hours or until cooked through. (The chicken is done when it is no longer pink inside and/or registers 165°F internally.)

4   Transfer the chicken to a cutting board and shred it or chop into bite-size pieces. Set aside.

5   Position the top oven rack about 6 inches below the broiler. Preheat the broiler. Line two baking sheets with parchment paper or foil (or line one pan and work in two batches).

6   Spread half the tortilla chips over each prepared pan. Top the chips with the shredded chicken, dividing it evenly, then sprinkle each pan evenly with 2 cups of the cheese.

(CONTINUES)

7   Broil the nachos, one pan at a time, for 2 to 3 minutes or until the cheese has fully melted.

8   Top the nachos as desired and serve immediately.

FREEZE FOR LATER: Follow step 1. Place the marinade and the chicken in a gallon-size freezer bag or container. Seal and freeze. Place the cheese in a quart-size freezer bag. Seal and freeze alongside the chicken.

PREPARE FROM FROZEN: *Note: You will need to have chips and your favorite toppings on hand to complete this meal.* Thaw. Transfer the chicken and marinade to the slow cooker. Follow steps 3 through 8.

Instant Pot • MAKES: 8 SERVINGS

MAKE IT NOW

1   In a small bowl, whisk together the cilantro, salsa, lime juice, garlic, cumin, salt, and red pepper flakes. *(Freezing instructions begin here.)*

2   Place the chicken in the 6-quart Instant Pot and pour the sauce over the top.

3   Lock and seal the lid. Cook at high pressure for 7 minutes, then quick release the pressure. (The chicken is done when it is no longer pink inside and/or register 165°F internally.)

4   Transfer the chicken to a cutting board and shred it or chop into bite-size pieces. Set aside.

5   Position the top oven rack about 6 inches below the broiler. Preheat the broiler. Line two baking sheets with parchment paper or foil (or line one pan and work in two batches).

6   Spread half the tortilla chips over each prepared pan. Top the chips with the shredded chicken, dividing it evenly, then sprinkle each pan evenly with 2 cups of the cheese.

7   Broil the nachos, one pan at a time, for 2 to 3 minutes or until the cheese has fully melted.

8   Top the nachos as desired and serve immediately.

FREEZE FOR LATER: Follow step 1. Place the marinade and the chicken in a gallon-size freezer bag or round container (do not stack the chicken breasts in the bag/container; instead, place them side by side). Seal and freeze. Place the cheese in a quart-size freezer bag. Seal and freeze alongside the chicken.

PREPARE FROM FROZEN: *Note: You will need to have chips and your favorite toppings on hand to complete this meal.* Thaw the cheese. Set the Instant Pot to "Sauté." Transfer the frozen meal to the pot and cook for 5 minutes to release some liquid. Press "Cancel." Follow step 3, but cook for 15 to 20 minutes. Follow steps 4 through 8.

Zesty Italian Shredded
Beef Subs, *page 133*

beef

SHREDDED BBQ BEEF SANDWICHES

Need a crowd-pleaser to feed a group with minimal fuss? This recipe has you covered. We've fed gaggles of college students, neighbors, and our own hungry families with this easy sweet-and-tangy shredded beef many times. With just a little prep on the front end, you'll have a fall-apart roast at the end of the day in your slow cooker or within minutes in your pot. For a more budget-friendly version, try our BBQ Pulled Pork Sandwiches (page 148).

1 teaspoon onion powder

1 teaspoon garlic powder

1 teaspoon salt

½ teaspoon ground black pepper

1 boneless beef chuck roast (about 3 pounds), trimmed of excess fat

1½ cups BBQ Sauce, homemade (see page 236) or your favorite all-natural store-bought BBQ sauce

8 to 10 whole-wheat hamburger buns

Slow Cooker • MAKES: 8 TO 10 SERVINGS

MAKE IT NOW

1 In a small bowl, combine the onion powder, garlic powder, salt, and pepper.

2 Pat the roast dry with paper towels and rub the seasoning mixture in on all sides. *(Freezing instructions begin here.)*

3 Place seasoned roast in the slow cooker and top with 1 cup of the BBQ sauce.

4 Cover and cook on Low for 8 to 10 hours or on High for 5 to 6 hours, until the meat easily shreds.

5 Transfer the roast to a cutting board and shred with two forks. Stir the meat back into the sauce.

6 Position the top oven rack about 6 inches below the broiler. Preheat the broiler.

7 Place the buns on a baking sheet with the insides facing up. Broil the buns for 1 to 2 minutes, until golden.

8 Using a slotted spoon, top each bun with some of the meat. Spoon over some of the remaining ½ cup BBQ sauce and enjoy.

FREEZE FOR LATER: Follow steps 1 and 2. Place the seasoned roast and 1 cup of the BBQ sauce in a gallon-size freezer bag or container. Seal and freeze. Pour the remaining ½ cup BBQ sauce into a small bag or container and seal. Freeze the sauce and the buns alongside the roast.

PREPARE FROM FROZEN: Thaw. Transfer the roast to the slow cooker. Follow steps 4 through 8.

Instant Pot • MAKES: 8 TO 10 SERVINGS

MAKE IT NOW

1   In the 6-quart Instant Pot, combine the onion powder, garlic powder, salt, and pepper.

2   Cut the meat into 2 × 2-inch pieces, trimming off excess fat as needed. Pat dry with a paper towel and add the meat to the Instant Pot with the seasoning mixture. Toss to coat. *(Freezing instructions begin here.)*

3   Pour 1 cup of the BBQ sauce over the meat. Stir to combine.

4   Lock and seal the lid. Cook at high pressure for 30 minutes. Allow the pressure to release naturally for 10 minutes, then quick release the remaining pressure.

5   Transfer the roast to a cutting board and shred with two forks. Stir the meat back into the sauce.

6   Position the top oven rack about 6 inches below the broiler. Preheat the broiler.

7   Place the buns on a baking sheet with the insides facing up. Broil the buns for 1 to 2 minutes, until golden.

8   Using a slotted spoon, top each bun with some of the meat. Spoon over some of the remaining ½ cup BBQ sauce and enjoy.

FREEZE FOR LATER: Follow steps 1 and 2. Place the seasoned meat and 1 cup of the BBQ sauce in a gallon-size freezer bag or round container. Seal and freeze (if using a freezer bag, set it in a bowl or round container with a diameter similar to the Instant Pot so it will fit in the pot when frozen; see page 22). Pour the remaining ½ cup BBQ sauce into a small bag or container and seal. Freeze the sauce and the buns alongside the meat.

PREPARE FROM FROZEN: Thaw the extra sauce and buns. Set the Instant Pot to "Sauté." Transfer the frozen meal to the pot and cook for 5 minutes to release some liquid. Press "Cancel." Follow steps 4 through 8.

WINE-BRAISED BRISKET
WITH CHIMICHURRI

Fall-apart-tender brisket meets a pop of freshness at the end in this recipe. The flavor and texture contrast of the braised meat topped with chimichurri sauce guarantees a full-flavored bite each time that's worthy of serving for a special occasion. Cooking brisket can be a little tricky, so it's important to know when it's properly cooked. A perfect slice should pull apart easily while maintaining good texture. An overcooked slice will fall apart when handled or moved. Note: You will not sear the brisket if making this as a freezer meal, but it still turned out delicious in our tests.

Chimichurri Sauce

⅔ cup loosely packed fresh parsley

⅔ cup loosely packed fresh cilantro

4 garlic cloves, peeled and left whole

¼ cup chopped red onion

¼ cup cider vinegar

1 teaspoon salt

¼ teaspoon red pepper flakes

¼ teaspoon ground black pepper

½ cup extra-virgin olive oil

Brisket

3 pounds beef brisket, trimmed of most fat

2 teaspoons salt

1 teaspoon ground black pepper

1 to 2 tablespoons avocado oil or olive oil

1 large yellow onion, coarsely chopped

2 celery stalks, chopped

6 garlic cloves, minced

1 teaspoon dried oregano

⅔ cup dry red wine (such as Cabernet Sauvignon)

½ cup beef broth

Slow Cooker • **MAKES: 6 SERVINGS**

MAKE IT NOW

1 *For the chimichurri sauce: (Freezing instructions begin here.)* In a food processor, combine the parsley, cilantro, garlic, onion, vinegar, salt, red pepper flakes, and black pepper and pulse until smooth. While pulsing, drizzle in the olive oil and pulse until well combined. Transfer the chimichurri to an airtight container and refrigerate.

2 *For the brisket:* Season each side of the brisket with ½ teaspoon of the salt and ¼ teaspoon of the black pepper.

(CONTINUES)

3   In a large skillet, heat the oil over medium-high heat until shimmery. Add the brisket and sear for 2 to 3 minutes per side, until browned on both sides. Transfer the brisket to the slow cooker.

4   In the same skillet, cook the onion and celery, stirring, until softened, about 4 minutes. Add the garlic and oregano and cook for about 1 minute more. Stir in the wine, broth, and the remaining 1 teaspoon salt and ½ teaspoon black pepper.

5   Carefully transfer the sauce to the slow cooker. The brisket should be nestled down in the sauce. Cover and cook on Low for 6 to 8 hours, until the brisket pulls apart easily but does not fall apart when handled.

6   Transfer the brisket to a cutting board, tent with foil, and let rest for 5 to 10 minutes. Set the chimichurri on the counter to come to room temperature.

7   Cut the brisket against the grain into ½-inch-thick slices. Fan out the slices on a serving platter, spoon some of the braising liquid over the meat, and drizzle the chimichurri over the top to serve.

FREEZE FOR LATER:

Chimichurri sauce: Follow step 1, omitting the vinegar (it will cause browning to occur in the freezer). Transfer the chimichurri to a quart-size freezer bag or container. Seal and freeze.

Brisket: Follow step 2. Place the seasoned brisket in a gallon-size freezer bag or container. (Do *not* sear the brisket before freezing it, as it is not safe to freeze partially cooked meat.) In a large skillet, heat the oil over medium-high heat and follow step 4. Allow the sauce to cool, then pour it over the brisket. Seal and freeze alongside the chimichurri.

PREPARE FROM FROZEN: *Note: You will need to have cider vinegar on hand to complete this meal.* Thaw. Stir the vinegar into the chimichurri and refrigerate. Follow steps 5 through 7.

Instant Pot • MAKES: 6 SERVINGS

MAKE IT NOW

1   *For the chimichurri sauce: (Freezing instructions begin here.)* In a food processor, combine the parsley, cilantro, garlic, onion, vinegar, salt, red pepper flakes, and black pepper and pulse until smooth. While pulsing,

drizzle in the olive oil and pulse until well combined. Transfer the chimichurri to an airtight container and refrigerate.

2   *For the brisket:* Season each side of the brisket with ½ teaspoon of the salt and ¼ teaspoon of the black pepper.

3   Set the 6-quart Instant Pot to "Sauté." Pour in the oil and heat until shimmery. Add the brisket and sear for about 3 minutes per side, until browned on both sides. Transfer the brisket to a plate and set aside.

4   Add the onion and celery to the pot and cook, stirring, until softened, about 4 minutes. Add the garlic and oregano and cook for about 1 minute more. Stir in the wine, broth, and remaining 1 teaspoon salt and ½ teaspoon black pepper. Press "Cancel."

5   Nestle the brisket into the sauce in the Instant Pot. Lock and seal the lid. Cook at high pressure for 50 minutes. Allow the pressure to release naturally for 10 minutes, then quick release the remaining pressure.

6   Transfer the brisket to a cutting board, tent with foil, and let rest for 5 to 10 minutes. Set the chimichurri on the counter to come to room temperature.

7   Cut the brisket against the grain into ½-inch-thick slices. Fan out the slices on a serving platter, spoon some of the braising liquid over the meat, and drizzle the chimichurri over the top to serve.

FREEZE FOR LATER:

Chimichurri sauce: Follow step 1, omitting the vinegar (it will cause browning to occur in the freezer). Transfer the chimichurri to a quart-size freezer bag or container. Seal and freeze.

Brisket: Follow step 2. Place the seasoned brisket in a gallon-size freezer bag or container. (Do *not* sear the brisket before freezing it, as it is not safe to freeze partially cooked meat.) In a large skillet, heat the oil over medium-high heat and follow step 4. Allow the sauce to cool, then pour it over the brisket. Seal and freeze alongside the chimichurri.

PREPARE FROM FROZEN*: *Note: You will need to have cider vinegar on hand to complete this meal.* Thaw. Stir the vinegar into the chimichurri and refrigerate. Follow steps 5 through 7.

We have found that this particular meal doesn't work as well when cooked straight from frozen in the Instant Pot. Because of this, we recommend thawing before cooking for best results.

MANCHOES

I have to give my husband credit for this recipe inspiration. He's been known to take almost any leftover meat and magically turn it into delicious nachos, which have become known as "Manchoes" in our house. While the name indicates a hearty meal, these shredded beef nachos can be lightened up as much as you want with fresh veggies on top, like lettuce, tomatoes, avocado, red onions, and more. That's the beauty of Manchoes. Customize them as much as you'd like! —Polly

1 boneless beef chuck roast (about 3 pounds), trimmed of excess fat

¼ cup taco seasoning, homemade (see page 243) or store-bought

1 cup salsa

½ cup low-sodium beef broth

1 (13-ounce) bag tortilla chips

4 cups shredded cheddar cheese

Optional toppings: diced avocado, salsa, chopped tomatoes, chopped fresh cilantro, black beans, sour cream, shredded lettuce, etc.

Slow Cooker • MAKES: 8 SERVINGS

MAKE IT NOW

1   Pat the roast dry with paper towels. Rub the taco seasoning all over the roast. *(Freezing instructions begin here.)*

2   Place the roast in the slow cooker. Top with the salsa and broth.

3   Cover and cook on Low for 8 to 10 hours, until the meat easily shreds. Transfer the roast to a cutting board and shred the meat with two forks. Set aside.

4   Preheat the broiler. Cover two baking sheets with parchment paper or foil for easy cleanup (or cover one pan and work in two batches).

5   Spread half the tortilla chips over each prepared pan. Top the chips on each pan evenly with the shredded meat. Then, top them evenly with the cheese.

6   Broil the nachos, one pan at a time, for 2 to 3 minutes, until the cheese has fully melted.

7   Top as desired and serve immediately.

(CONTINUES)

FREEZE FOR LATER: Follow step 1. Place the seasoned roast in a gallon-size freezer bag or container. Add the salsa and broth. Seal and freeze. Place the cheese in a separate bag or container. Seal and freeze alongside the roast.

PREPARE FROM FROZEN: *Note: You will need to have tortilla chips and your desired toppings on hand to finish this meal.* Thaw. Place the roast and sauce in the slow cooker. Follow steps 3 through 7.

Instant Pot • MAKES: 8 SERVINGS

MAKE IT NOW

1   Pat the roast dry. Cut the meat into 2 × 2-inch pieces (trimming off fat) and season with the taco seasoning. *(Freezing instructions begin here.)*

2   Place the meat, salsa, and broth in the 6-quart Instant Pot.

3   Lock and seal the lid. Cook at high pressure for 30 minutes with a 10-minute natural release and then quick release of the pressure. Transfer the roast to a cutting board and shred the meat with two forks. Set aside.

4   Preheat the broiler. Cover two baking sheets with parchment paper or foil for easy cleanup (or cover one pan and work in two batches).

5   Spread half the tortilla chips over each prepared pan. Top the chips on each pan evenly with the shredded meat. Then, top them evenly with the cheese.

6   Broil the nachos, one pan at a time, for 2 to 3 minutes, until the cheese has fully melted.

7   Top as desired and serve immediately.

FREEZE FOR LATER: Follow step 1. Place the seasoned roast in a gallon-size freezer bag or container. Add the salsa and broth. Seal and freeze (if using a freezer bag, set it in a bowl or round container with a diameter similar to the Instant Pot so it will fit in the pot when frozen; see page 22). Place the cheese in a separate bag or container. Seal and freeze alongside the roast.

PREPARE FROM FROZEN: *Note: You will need to have tortilla chips and your desired toppings on hand to finish this meal.* Set the Instant Pot to "Sauté." Transfer the frozen meal to the pot and cook for 5 minutes to release some liquid. Press "Cancel." Follow steps 3 through 7. (The frozen meat will cook in the same amount of time as fresh.)

BALSAMIC SHREDDED BEEF

I've been making this drop-and-go shredded beef for my family for years. It's one of those dinners where no one complains. (High fives!) The juices left in the cooker are perfect for dipping sandwiches in, or you can thicken them up at the end to serve as a gravy with the meat and poured over mashed potatoes or polenta. Expect a little sweetness in the sauce and a hint of heat in the background. Our recipe testing team loved it and found that if you marinate the meat in the sauce overnight or freeze it in the sauce, the flavor is even better. —Rachel

1 cup beef broth

¼ cup balsamic vinegar

2 tablespoons low-sodium soy sauce

2 tablespoons honey

4 garlic cloves, minced

½ teaspoon red pepper flakes

1 boneless beef chuck roast (about 3 pounds), trimmed of excess fat

Salt and ground black pepper

2 tablespoons cornstarch (optional)

Slow Cooker • **MAKES: 6 TO 8 SERVINGS**

MAKE IT NOW

1   In a small bowl, whisk together the broth, vinegar, soy sauce, honey, garlic, and red pepper flakes.

2   Season the roast lightly with salt and pepper on all sides. *(Freezing instructions begin here.)*

3   Place the roast in the slow cooker and pour the sauce over the top. Cover and cook on Low for 8 to 10 hours or on High for 5 to 6 hours, until the meat easily shreds.

4   Transfer the roast to a cutting board and shred the meat with two forks.

5   If you'd like to thicken the sauce, in a small bowl, stir together the cornstarch and 2 tablespoons water until smooth. Carefully pour or ladle the juices from the slow cooker into a medium saucepan and add the cornstarch mixture. Bring to a boil over high heat. Reduce the heat to maintain a simmer and cook, stirring, until thickened, about 3 minutes. Pour the sauce back into the slow cooker.

6   Stir the shredded meat into the sauce and serve warm.

(CONTINUES)

FREEZE FOR LATER: Follow steps 1 and 2. Place the roast in a gallon-size freezer bag or container and pour in the sauce. Seal and freeze.

PREPARE FROM FROZEN: *Note: You may want to have (optional) cornstarch on hand to complete this meal.* Thaw. Follow steps 3 through 6.

Instant Pot • MAKES: 6 TO 8 SERVINGS

MAKE IT NOW

1   In a small bowl, whisk together the broth, vinegar, soy sauce, honey, garlic, and red pepper flakes.

2   Cut the meat into 2 × 2-inch pieces, trimming off excess fat as needed. Pat dry with a paper towel and season lightly with salt and pepper. *(Freezing instructions begin here.)*

3   Place the meat and sauce in the 6-quart Instant Pot. Lock and seal the lid. Cook at high pressure for 30 minutes. Allow the pressure to release naturally for 10 minutes, then quick release the remaining pressure.

4   Transfer the roast to a cutting board and shred the meat with two forks.

5   If you'd like to thicken the sauce, in a small bowl, stir together the cornstarch and 2 tablespoons water until smooth. Set the Instant Pot to "Sauté." Stir the cornstarch mixture into the sauce and bring to a boil. Cook, stirring, until thickened, about 3 minutes. Press "Cancel."

6   Stir the shredded meat into the sauce and serve warm.

FREEZE FOR LATER: Follow steps 1 and 2. Place the meat in a gallon-size freezer bag or round container and pour in the sauce. Seal and freeze (if using a freezer bag, set it in a bowl or round container with a diameter similar to the Instant Pot so it will fit in the pot when frozen; see page 22).

PREPARE FROM FROZEN: *Note: You may want to have (optional) cornstarch on hand to complete this meal.* Set the Instant Pot to "Sauté." Transfer the frozen meal to the pot and cook for 5 minutes to release some liquid. Press "Cancel." Follow steps 3 through 6. (The frozen meat will cook in the same amount of time as fresh.)

ASIAN-STYLE BEEF SHORT RIBS

Braised beef short ribs make for one of the most meltingly tender, fall-off-the-bone pot roasts imaginable. The complex, sweet-spicy combo of flavors in this Asian-inspired dish may lead you to believe it's a high-maintenance recipe. However, you'll be happy to know that it comes together fairly quickly. Serve these ribs over a bed of rice, mashed potatoes, or polenta, with extra sauce on top. This is a more expensive cut of beef, so either look for a sale or ask the butcher for a bulk discount.

Shortcut: *Ask your butcher to trim the ribs of excess fat and cut them into 2-inch pieces for you.*

½ cup low-sodium soy sauce

½ cup low-sodium beef broth

¼ cup honey

1 tablespoon minced fresh ginger

1 teaspoon sesame oil

4 garlic cloves, minced

½ teaspoon ground black pepper

½ teaspoon red pepper flakes (or up to 1 teaspoon if you like more heat)

¾ cup sliced green onions, plus more for garnish

5 pounds bone-in English-style beef short ribs, trimmed of excess fat and cut crosswise into 2-inch pieces

2 tablespoons cornstarch

1 teaspoon sesame seeds

Slow Cooker • MAKES: 5 OR 6 SERVINGS

MAKE IT NOW

1   In a medium bowl, whisk together the soy sauce, broth, honey, ginger, sesame oil, garlic, black pepper, red pepper flakes, and green onions. *(Freezing instructions begin here.)*

2   Place the ribs and sauce in the slow cooker and stir to coat the ribs. Cover and cook on Low for 8 to 10 hours, until the meat falls off the bone. (If you're able to, give the ribs a stir halfway through the cooking time for more even cooking.) Use tongs to transfer the ribs to a serving platter.

3   Carefully pour or ladle the juices from the slow cooker into a medium saucepan. In a small bowl, stir together the cornstarch and 2 tablespoons water until smooth. Add the cornstarch mixture to the pan and stir to combine. Bring to a boil over high heat. Reduce the heat to maintain a simmer and cook, stirring, until thickened, about 3 minutes.

(CONTINUES)

4   Drizzle some of the thickened sauce over the ribs and garnish with the sesame seeds and green onions. Serve warm with extra sauce on the side.

FREEZE FOR LATER: Follow step 1. Place the ribs and sauce in one or two gallon-size freezer bags or containers. Seal and freeze.

PREPARE FROM FROZEN: *Note: You will need cornstarch and sesame seeds on hand to complete this meal.* Thaw. Follow steps 2 through 4.

Instant Pot • MAKES: 5 OR 6 SERVINGS

MAKE IT NOW

1   In a medium bowl, whisk together the soy sauce, broth, honey, ginger, sesame oil, garlic, black pepper, red pepper flakes, and green onions. *(Freezing instructions begin here.)*

2   Place the ribs and marinade in the 6-quart Instant Pot and stir to coat the ribs. Lock and seal the lid. Cook at high pressure for 40 minutes. Allow the pressure to release naturally for 10 minutes (or longer, if you prefer), then quick release the remaining pressure. Use tongs to transfer the ribs to a serving platter.

3   Set the Instant Pot to "Sauté." In a small bowl, stir together the cornstarch and 2 tablespoons water until smooth. Stir the cornstarch mixture into the sauce in the pot and bring to a boil. Cook, stirring, until thickened, about 3 minutes. Press "Cancel."

4   Drizzle some of the thickened sauce over the ribs and garnish with the sesame seeds and green onions. Serve warm with extra sauce on the side.

FREEZE FOR LATER: Follow step 1. Place the ribs and sauce in one or two gallon-size freezer bags or containers.

PREPARE FROM FROZEN*: *Note: You will need cornstarch and sesame seeds on hand to complete this meal.* Thaw. Follow steps 2 through 4.

*We have found that this recipe cooks unevenly from frozen in the Instant Pot. Because of this, we recommend thawing before cooking for best results.

EASY-PEASY PESTO MEATBALL SUBS

These hearty, cheesy sandwiches get two thumbs-ups from all of our family members. Keep frozen meatballs on hand so you can whip up this tasty crowd-pleaser anytime. If you're using store-bought pesto, the refrigerated version has much more flavor than the jarred kind. But we'll always make a case for using our homemade pesto and, for that matter, our Marvelous Marinara Sauce (page 216), too. Make a large batch of both and freeze them to have on hand!

Cooking Tip: *Broiling, browning, or baking the meatballs before cooking them in the slow cooker or Instant Pot helps render fat from them, adds flavor, and avoids a greasy outcome at the end.*

1 pound lean ground beef or lean ground turkey

⅔ cup whole-wheat panko bread crumbs

⅔ cup pesto, homemade (see page 239) or store-bought (see headnote)

¼ cup grated Parmesan cheese

1 large egg, beaten

1 to 2 tablespoons avocado oil or olive oil (for Instant Pot only)

2 (24-ounce) jars marinara sauce, or 6 cups Marvelous Marinara Sauce (page 216)

Salt and ground black pepper

6 whole-wheat hoagie rolls

12 slices provolone or mozzarella cheese

Slow Cooker • MAKES: 6 HOAGIE SANDWICHES (ABOUT 18 MEATBALLS)

MAKE IT NOW

1   In a large bowl, combine the beef, bread crumbs, pesto, Parmesan, and egg. Mix well using your hands. Shape the mixture into about eighteen 2-inch-diameter meatballs. *(Freezing instructions begin here.)*

2   Position the top oven rack about 6 inches below the broiler. Preheat the broiler. Line a rimmed baking sheet with foil.

3   Place the meatballs on the prepared baking sheet* and broil for 4 to 5 minutes, until the meatballs are browned on the outside and their fat is rendered (the meatballs will not be cooked through at this point).

If you'd like, you can place a wire rack on top of the rimmed baking sheet and bake the meatballs on top to allow the grease to drip below.

(CONTINUES)

4   Transfer the meatballs to the slow cooker, pour in the marinara, and stir to coat. Evenly distribute the meatballs over the bottom of the cooker. Cover and cook on Low for 4 to 6 hours, until the meatballs are tender. Use a large spoon to skim any grease from the surface. Season with salt and pepper.

5   Position the top oven rack about 6 inches below the broiler. Preheat the broiler.

6   Place the rolls on a baking sheet with the insides facing up. Broil the rolls for 1 to 2 minutes, until golden. Watch carefully so they do not burn.

7   Remove the rolls from the broiler and top each roll with 3 meatballs, a spoonful or two of sauce, and 2 slices of provolone. Broil the sandwiches for a few minutes more, until the cheese has melted. Serve immediately.

FREEZE FOR LATER:

Method 1: *Uncooked Meatballs:* Follow step 1. Place the uncooked meatballs on a rimmed baking sheet and freeze for an hour or so, until solid. Dump the meatballs into a gallon-size freezer bag or container. Seal and freeze. Place the buns and provolone or mozzarella in separate freezer bags. If using homemade marinara (instead of jarred), pour into a separate freezer bag, too. Seal and freeze alongside the meatballs.

Method 2: *Cooked Meatballs in Sauce:* Preheat the oven to 350°F. Line a rimmed baking sheet with foil. Follow step 1. Place the meatballs on the prepared baking sheet.* Bake for about 25 minutes, until the internal temperature reaches 160°F. (It is *not* safe to partially cook meat and freeze it for later, so it's important to fully cook the meatballs before freezing them.) Let cool. Transfer the cooled meatballs to a gallon-size freezer bag or container and pour in the marinara. Seal and freeze. Place the buns and provolone or mozzarella in separate freezer bags. Seal and freeze alongside the meatballs.

If you'd like, you can place a wire rack on top of the rimmed baking sheet and bake the meatballs on top to allow the grease to drip below.

PREPARE FROM FROZEN: *Note: You will need to have salt and pepper on hand to complete this meal.*

Uncooked Meatballs: *Note: You will need to have marinara sauce on hand to complete this meal, if it's not already frozen along with the meal.* Thaw. Follow steps 2 through 7.

Cooked Meatballs in Sauce: Thaw. Follow step 4, but cook on Low for up to 4 hours. Follow steps 5 through 7.

(CONTINUES)

Instant Pot •

MAKE IT NOW

1   In a large bowl, combine the beef, bread crumbs, pesto, Parmesan, and egg. Mix well using your hands. Shape the mixture into about eighteen 2-inch diameter meatballs. *(Freezing instructions begin here.)*

2   Set the 6-quart Instant Pot to "Sauté." Pour the oil into the pot and heat until shimmery. Working in batches, brown the meatballs on all sides, 5 minutes or so. Press "Cancel." Transfer the meatballs to a paper towel–lined plate and wipe out any grease from the pot.

3   Place the meatballs back into the Instant Pot, pour in the marinara, and gently stir to coat.

4   Lock and seal the lid. Cook at high pressure for 5 minutes, then quick release the pressure. (The meatballs are done when they register 160°F internally.) Use a large spoon to skim any grease from the surface. Season with salt and pepper.

5   Position the top oven rack about 6 inches below the broiler. Preheat the broiler.

6   Place the rolls on a baking sheet with the insides facing up. Broil the rolls for 1 to 2 minutes, until golden. Watch carefully so they do not burn.

7   Remove the rolls from the broiler and top each roll with 3 meatballs, a spoonful or two of sauce, and 2 slices of provolone. Broil the sandwiches for a few minutes more, until the cheese has melted. Serve immediately.

FREEZE FOR LATER: Preheat the oven to 350°F. Line a rimmed baking sheet with foil. Follow step 1. Place the meatballs on the prepared baking sheet. Bake for about 25 minutes, until the internal temperature reaches 160°F. (It is *not* safe to partially cook meat and freeze it for later, so it's important to fully cook the meatballs before freezing them.) Let cool. Transfer the cooled meatballs to a gallon-size freezer bag and pour in the marinara. Seal and freeze. Place the buns and provolone or mozzarella in separate freezer bags. Seal and freeze alongside the meatballs.

PREPARE FROM FROZEN: *Note: You will need to have salt and pepper on hand to complete this meal.* Thaw the buns and provolone or mozzarella. Set the Instant Pot to "Sauté." Transfer the frozen meal to the pot and cook for 5 minutes to release some liquid. Press "Cancel." Follow step 4, but cook for 3 to 5 minutes, until the meatballs are warmed through. Follow steps 5 through 7.

THE HUMBLE HOME COOK'S BEEF BOURGUIGNON

Thank you to one of my heroes, Mrs. Julia Child, for giving me the confidence as a humble home cook to tweak this classic French recipe for the slow cooker and pressure cooker. I substituted the traditional pearl onions for an American favorite, baby potatoes. The red wine, soy sauce, tomato paste, and mushrooms add a deep savory meatiness to the sauce (or is it a gravy?). The end result is a velvety, rich dish that is melt-in-your-mouth divine. —Rachel

4 thick-cut slices bacon, finely chopped

1 large onion, finely chopped

Salt and ground black pepper

3 garlic cloves, minced

¼ cup unbleached all-purpose flour or white whole-wheat flour

1½ cups dry red wine (we recommend Pinot Noir)

1½ cups low-sodium chicken broth, homemade (see page 240) or store-bought

2 tablespoons tomato paste

¼ cup low-sodium soy sauce

2 sprigs fresh thyme, or ½ teaspoon ground thyme

1 bay leaf

8 ounces button mushrooms, quartered

5 medium carrots, sliced on an angle about ½ inch thick (about 2 cups)

1 pound baby Yukon Gold potatoes, cut into 1-inch pieces (5 to 6 cups)

1 boneless beef chuck roast (about 3 pounds), trimmed and cut into 1½-inch chunks

Chopped fresh parsley, for garnish

Slow Cooker • MAKES: 8 SERVINGS

MAKE IT NOW

1   In a large skillet, fry the bacon over medium-high heat until crisp. Using a slotted spoon, transfer the bacon to the slow cooker, leaving the bacon grease in the pan.

2   Add the onion to the pan with the bacon grease and cook, stirring, until softened, about 4 minutes, seasoning lightly with salt and pepper as it cooks and stirring in the garlic during the last 30 to 60 seconds of cooking. Add the flour and cook, stirring, for 1 to 2 minutes. Add the wine, broth, tomato paste, and soy sauce and whisk until smooth, scraping up the browned bits from the bottom of the pan. Bring to a simmer and cook for about 2 minutes, until thickened slightly. *(Freezing instructions begin here.)*

(CONTINUES)

3   Pour the sauce into the slow cooker. Stir in the thyme, bay leaf, mushrooms, carrots, and potatoes.

4   Season the beef liberally with salt and pepper on all sides, add it to the cooker, and stir to combine.

5   Cover and cook on Low for 8 to 10 hours, until the beef and vegetables are very tender.

6   Discard the bay leaf and thyme sprigs. Use a large spoon to skim some of the fat off the surface, if desired. Taste and season with salt and pepper. Garnish with parsley and serve.

FREEZE FOR LATER: Follow steps 1 and 2, but transfer the bacon to a paper towel-lined plate. Let the bacon and sauce cool, then transfer both to one or two gallon-size freezer bags or containers. If using just one bag, it should fit but be very full, so have someone help hold it open while filling it. Season the beef liberally with salt and pepper on all sides. Place the seasoned beef, thyme, bay leaf, mushrooms, carrots, and potatoes in the same bag or container as the bacon and sauce. Seal and toss gently to combine, making sure the potatoes are completely submerged in the sauce to prevent browning. Freeze.

PREPARE FROM FROZEN: *Note: Have salt, pepper, and parsley to complete this meal.* Thaw. Transfer to the slow cooker and follow steps 5 and 6.

Instant Pot • MAKES: 8 SERVINGS

MAKE IT NOW

1   Place the bacon in the 6-quart Instant Pot and set the pot to "Sauté." Fry the bacon until crisp on both sides. Using a slotted spoon, transfer the bacon to a paper towel–lined plate, leaving the bacon grease in the pot.

2   Add the onion to the pot and cook, stirring, until softened, about 4 minutes, seasoning lightly with salt and pepper as it cooks and stirring in the garlic during the last 30 to 60 seconds of cooking. Add the flour and cook, stirring, for 1 to 2 minutes. Add the wine, broth, tomato paste, and soy sauce and whisk until smooth, scraping up the browned bits from the bottom of the pot. Bring to a simmer and cook for about 2 minutes, until thickened slightly. Press "Cancel." *(Freezing instructions begin here.)*

(CONTINUES)

3   Add the thyme, bay leaf, mushrooms, carrots, and potatoes to the pot and stir to combine. Season the beef liberally with salt and pepper on all sides, add it to the pot, and stir to combine.

4   Lock and seal the lid. Cook at high pressure for 30 minutes. Allow the pressure to release naturally for 10 minutes, then quick release the remaining pressure.

5   Discard the bay leaf and thyme sprigs. Use a large spoon to skim some of the fat off the surface, if desired. Taste and season with salt and pepper. Garnish with parsley and serve.

FREEZE FOR LATER: Follow steps 1 and 2. Let the bacon and sauce cool, then transfer both to one or two gallon-size bags or round containers. If using just one bag, it should fit but be very full, so have someone help hold it open while filling it. Season the beef liberally with salt and pepper on all sides. Place the seasoned beef, thyme, bay leaf, mushrooms, carrots, and potatoes in the same bag or container as the bacon and sauce. Seal and toss gently to combine, making sure the potatoes are completely submerged in the sauce to prevent browning. Freeze (if using a freezer bag, set it in a bowl or round container with a diameter similar to the Instant Pot so it will fit in the pot when frozen; see page 22).

PREPARE FROM FROZEN: *Note: Have salt, pepper, and parsley on hand to complete this meal.* Set the Instant Pot to "Sauté." Transfer the frozen meal to the pot and cook for 5 minutes to release some liquid (or until it cooks down enough to close the lid). Press "Cancel." Follow steps 4 and 5. (The frozen meat will cook in the same amount of time as fresh.)

ZESTY ITALIAN SHREDDED BEEF SUBS

Contributed by Whitney Reist of Sweet Cayenne

This recipe is part of my "back-pocket recipe collection" because I know I can rely on it to feed a lot of people at a moment's notice while leaving them happy and satisfied! It's been my go-to for game-day menus, small group gatherings at church, family vacations, and freezer prep for my husband when I'm planning to be away. Even though these subs can serve a lot of people at one time, I love to freeze the fully cooked meat in smaller portions for two people so that my husband and I have something delicious waiting in the freezer when we need dinner in a pinch! Look for the jarred Italian-style giardiniera vegetable mix, a combo of pickled veggies like peppers, celery, cauliflower, and more, in the pickle aisle.

1 tablespoon Italian seasoning

1 teaspoon salt

1 teaspoon lemon pepper seasoning

¾ teaspoon garlic powder

½ teaspoon onion powder

¼ teaspoon red pepper flakes (or ½ teaspoon if you like a noticeable kick of heat)

1 boneless beef chuck roast (about 3 pounds), trimmed of excess fat

1 (16-ounce) jar deli-sliced pepperoncini peppers, drained, 3 tablespoons liquid from the jar reserved

1 (16-ounce) jar Italian-style giardiniera vegetable mix, drained

2 cups low-sodium beef broth (we recommend Kitchen Basics)

8 to 10 (6-inch) whole-wheat sub rolls or ciabatta rolls

8 to 10 slices provolone cheese

Slow Cooker • MAKES: 8 TO 10 SERVINGS

MAKE IT NOW

1   In a small bowl, combine the Italian seasoning, salt, lemon pepper, garlic powder, onion powder, and red pepper flakes.

2   Pat the roast dry with paper towels and rub the seasoning blend over all sides of the roast. *(Freezing instructions begin here.)*

3   Place the roast in the slow cooker. Add the pepperoncini peppers, pepperoncini liquid, giardiniera vegetables, and broth.

(CONTINUES)

4   Cover and cook on Low for 8 to 10 hours or on High for 5 to 6 hours, until the meat easily shreds.

5   When the roast is done, preheat the oven to 350°F.

6   Wrap the rolls in foil, place them on a rimmed baking sheet, and warm them in the oven for 8 minutes. Remove the rolls from the oven and switch the oven to broil on low.

7   Transfer the roast to a cutting board and shred with two forks. Return the meat to the cooker and stir to combine.

8   Unwrap the rolls and use a slotted spoon to top them with the shredded beef and vegetables. Top each roll with a slice of provolone. Broil the subs for 2 to 3 minutes to melt the cheese.

9   Serve the subs immediately, with the juices from the slow cooker in small bowls alongside for dipping. Enjoy!

FREEZE FOR LATER: Follow steps 1 and 2. Place the seasoned roast, pepperoncini peppers, pepperoncini juice, giardiniera vegetables, and broth in a gallon-size freezer bag or container. Seal and freeze. Place the rolls and cheese in separate freezer bags. Seal and freeze alongside the roast.

PREPARE FROM FROZEN: Thaw. Place the roast and juices in the slow cooker. Follow steps 4 through 9.

Instant Pot • MAKES: 8 TO 10 SERVINGS

MAKE IT NOW

1   In a small bowl, combine the Italian seasoning, salt, lemon pepper, garlic powder, onion powder, and red pepper flakes.

2   Cut the beef into 2 × 2-inch chunks, trimming off excess fat as needed, and pat dry with paper towels. Place the beef in the 6-quart Instant Pot, sprinkle the spice mixture over the beef, and toss to combine, coating all sides.

3   Add the pepperoncini peppers, pepperoncini juice, giardiniera vegetables, and broth to the pot. *(Freezing instructions begin here.)*

4   Lock and seal the lid. Cook at high pressure for 30 minutes. Allow the pressure to release naturally for 10 minutes, then quick release the remaining pressure.

5   Meanwhile, preheat the oven to 350°F.

6   Wrap the rolls in foil, place them on a rimmed baking sheet, and warm them in the oven for 8 minutes. Remove the rolls from the oven and switch the oven to broil.

7   Using a slotted spoon, transfer the beef to a cutting board and shred with two forks. Return the meat to the pot and stir to combine.

8   Unwrap the rolls and use a slotted spoon to top them with the shredded beef and vegetables. Top each roll with a slice of provolone. Broil the subs for 2 to 3 minutes to melt the cheese.

9   Serve the subs immediately, with the juices from the pot in small bowls alongside for dipping. Enjoy!

FREEZE FOR LATER: Follow steps 1 through 3. Transfer the meat mixture to a gallon-size freezer bag or round container. Seal and freeze (if using a freezer bag, set it in a bowl or round container with a diameter similar to the Instant Pot so it will fit in the pot when frozen; see page 22). Place the rolls and cheese in separate freezer bags. Seal and freeze alongside the meat mixture.

PREPARE FROM FROZEN: Thaw the rolls and cheese. Set the Instant Pot to "Sauté." Transfer the frozen meal to the pot and cook for 5 minutes to release some liquid. Press "Cancel." Follow steps 4 through 9. (The frozen meat will cook in the same amount of time as fresh.)

FRENCH DIP GRILLED CHEESE SANDWICHES

Everyone loves grilled cheese, so why not make it even more irresistible? This upgraded version is easy to throw together: Just toss a simple marinade and the roast in the cooker. You'll end up with fall-apart beef and an au jus you may just want to drink. Then, with just a few minutes of work at the end, say hello to melty, ooey-gooey, meaty sandwiches to dip in that luxurious sauce.

3 cups low-sodium beef broth

2 tablespoons low-sodium soy sauce

1 tablespoon dried minced onion

1 teaspoon garlic powder

½ teaspoon salt, plus more as needed

½ teaspoon ground black pepper, plus more as needed

½ teaspoon dried oregano

¼ teaspoon ground thyme

1 bay leaf

Pinch of red pepper flakes

1 boneless beef chuck roast (about 3 pounds), trimmed of excess fat

4 to 6 tablespoons (½ to ¾ stick) butter, at room temperature

12 to 16 slices sourdough bread

12 to 16 slices provolone, cheddar, mozzarella, or pepper Jack cheese

---

Slow Cooker • MAKES: 6 TO 8 LARGE SANDWICHES

MAKE IT NOW

1   In a small bowl, whisk together the broth, soy sauce, minced onion, garlic powder, salt, black pepper, oregano, thyme, bay leaf, and red pepper flakes. *(Freezing instructions begin here.)*

2   Place the roast in the cooker and season lightly with salt and black pepper on all sides. Pour the sauce over the top.

3   Cover and cook on Low for 8 to 10 hours or on High for 5 to 6 hours, until the meat easily shreds. Transfer the roast to a cutting board and shred with two forks. Return the meat to the cooker and stir it into the sauce.

4   Spread a thin layer of butter over one side of each slice of bread. Place a slice of cheese on the unbuttered side of half the slices of bread. Using a slotted spoon, add a layer of the shredded meat (be sure to drain the liquid first). Top with another slice of cheese and a second slice of bread, buttered-side up.

5   Heat a large skillet or griddle over medium heat. Cook the sandwiches for a few minutes on each side, until the bread is golden brown and the cheese has melted.

6   Serve the sandwiches warm, with the warmed juices from the cooker in small bowls alongside for dipping.

FREEZE FOR LATER: Follow step 1. Pour the sauce into a gallon-size freezer bag or container. Season the roast lightly with salt and black pepper and add to the bag/container with the sauce. Seal and freeze. Place the bread and cheese in separate freezer bags or containers. Seal and freeze alongside the roast.

PREPARE FROM FROZEN: *Note: You will need to have butter on hand to complete this meal.* Thaw. Place in the slow cooker. Follow steps 3 through 6.

Instant Pot • MAKES: 6 TO 8 LARGE SANDWICHES

MAKE IT NOW

1   In a small bowl, whisk together the broth, soy sauce, minced onion, garlic powder, salt, black pepper, oregano, thyme, bay leaf, and red pepper flakes.

2   Cut the meat into 2 × 2-inch pieces, trimming off excess fat as needed. Pat dry with paper towels and season lightly with salt and black pepper on all sides. *(Freezing instructions begin here.)*

3   Place the beef in the 6-quart Instant Pot and pour in the sauce.

4   Lock and seal the lid. Cook at high pressure for 30 minutes. Allow the pressure to release naturally for 10 minutes, then quick release the remaining pressure. Using a slotted spoon, transfer the roast to a cutting board and shred with two forks. Return the meat to the pot and stir it into the sauce.

5   Spread a thin layer of butter over one side of each slice of bread. Place a slice of cheese on the unbuttered side of half the slices of bread. Using a slotted spoon, add a layer of the shredded meat (be sure to drain the liquid first). Top with another slice of cheese and a second slice of bread, buttered-side up.

6   Heat a large skillet or griddle over medium heat. Cook the sandwiches for a few minutes on each side, until the bread is golden brown and the cheese has melted.

7   Serve the sandwiches warm, with the warmed juices from the cooker in small bowls alongside for dipping.

(CONTINUES)

FREEZE FOR LATER: Follow steps 1 and 2. Place the sauce and the meat in a gallon-size freezer bag or round container. Seal and freeze (if using a freezer bag, set it in a bowl or round container with a diameter similar to the Instant Pot so it will fit in the pot when frozen; see page 22). Place the bread and cheese in separate freezer bags or containers. Seal and freeze alongside the meat.

PREPARE FROM FROZEN: *Note: You will need to have butter on hand to complete this meal.* Thaw the bread and cheese. Set the Instant Pot to "Sauté." Transfer the frozen meat to the pot and cook for 5 minutes to release some liquid. Press "Cancel." Follow steps 4 through 7. (The frozen meat will cook in the same amount of time as fresh.)

MOUTH-WATERING BRISKET
WITH BALSAMIC GLAZE
Contributed by Molly Stillman of Still Being Molly

Our family loves beef, and this mouth-watering savory brisket with just a hint of sweetness wins my family (and especially my husband) over every time. The ingredients in this recipe are basic (and you probably have most of them on hand already!), it requires very little prep (it's pretty much a drop-and-go!), and it will impress your family or guests. Be sure to save the juices for the leftovers, because this brisket only gets better with time. And don't skimp on drizzling the sauce at the end, because that is most definitely the best part!

Shortcut: *You can find premade balsamic glaze in the vinegar aisle. Look for the one with the fewest ingredients.*

¼ cup avocado oil or olive oil

⅓ cup balsamic vinegar

¼ cup dry red wine (optional)

¼ cup Balsamic Glaze (recipe follows)

1 tablespoon honey or pure maple syrup

6 garlic cloves, minced

4 teaspoons salt

1½ teaspoons ground black pepper

1 teaspoon onion powder

3 bay leaves

3 pounds beef brisket, trimmed of most fat

2 tablespoons cornstarch (optional)

Slow Cooker • MAKES: 6 SERVINGS

MAKE IT NOW

1   In a medium bowl, whisk together the oil, vinegar, wine (if using), balsamic glaze, honey, garlic, salt, pepper, and onion powder. Add the bay leaves. *(Freezing instructions begin here.)* (At this point, you can transfer this sauce to a large bowl or freezer bag, add the brisket, seal, and marinate overnight in the refrigerator, if you'd like.)

2   Place the brisket in the slow cooker and pour in the sauce.

3   Cover and cook on Low for 6 to 8 hours, until the brisket pulls apart easily but does not fall apart when handled.

4   Transfer the brisket to a cutting board, tent with foil, and let rest for 5 to 10 minutes.

(CONTINUES)

5   If you'd like to thicken the sauce, in a small bowl, stir together the cornstarch and 2 tablespoons water until smooth. Set a strainer over a medium saucepan and carefully strain the juices from the cooker into the pan. Whisk in the cornstarch mixture and bring to a boil over high heat. Reduce the heat to maintain a simmer and cook, whisking, until thickened, about 3 minutes.

6   Cut the brisket against the grain into ½-inch-thick slices. Fan them out on a serving platter and spoon some of the sauce over the top. Serve the rest of the sauce on the side.

FREEZE FOR LATER: Follow step 1. Pour the sauce into a gallon-size freezer bag or container and add the brisket. Seal and freeze.

PREPARE FROM FROZEN: *Note: You may want to have (optional) cornstarch on hand to complete this meal.* Thaw. Place in the slow cooker. Follow steps 3 through 6.

Instant Pot • MAKES: 6 SERVINGS

MAKE IT NOW

1   In a medium bowl, whisk together the oil, vinegar, wine (if using), balsamic glaze, honey, garlic, salt, pepper, and onion powder. Add the bay leaves. *(Freezing instructions begin here.)* (At this point, you can transfer this sauce to a large bowl or freezer bag, add the brisket, seal, and marinate overnight in the refrigerator, if you'd like.)

2   Place the brisket in the 6-quart Instant Pot and pour in the sauce.

3   Lock and seal the lid. Cook at high pressure for 50 minutes. Allow the pressure to release naturally for 10 minutes, then quick release the remaining pressure.

4   Transfer the brisket to a cutting board, tent with foil, and let rest for 5 to 10 minutes.

5   If you'd like to thicken the sauce, in a small bowl, stir together the cornstarch and 2 tablespoons water until smooth. Set the Instant Pot to "Sauté." Whisk the cornstarch mixture into the sauce and bring to a boil over high heat. Cook, whisking, until thickened, about 3 minutes. Press "Cancel."

6   Cut the brisket against the grain into ½-inch-thick slices. Fan them out on a serving platter and spoon some of the sauce over the top. Serve the rest of the sauce on the side.

FREEZE FOR LATER: Follow step 1. Place the sauce and the brisket in a gallon-size freezer bag or container. Seal and freeze (if using a freezer bag, set it in a bowl or round container with a diameter similar to the Instant Pot so it will fit in the pot when frozen; see page 22).

PREPARE FROM FROZEN*: *Note: You may want to have (optional) cornstarch on hand to complete this meal.* Thaw. Place in the Instant Pot. Follow steps 3 through 6.

*We have found that this particular meal isn't nearly as good when cooked straight from frozen in the Instant Pot. Because of this, we recommend thawing before cooking for best results.

BALSAMIC GLAZE
MAKES: GENEROUS ¼ CUP

½ cup balsamic vinegar

3 tablespoons honey or pure maple syrup

In a small saucepan, whisk together the balsamic vinegar and honey. Heat over medium heat until the mixture begins to bubble, then reduce the heat to medium-low and simmer until reduced by half, about 13 minutes. You'll know it's ready when the mixture coats the back of a spoon. Set aside to cool. It will thicken even more as it sits. Use right away or store in the refrigerator until ready to use.

SHREDDED BEEF AND CHEESE TAQUITOS

This large-batch recipe will feed your family tonight *and* likely provide a second batch for the freezer for those busy weeknights when you're on the go. The beauty of beef taquitos (just like our chicken version on page 52) is that they can be baked straight from frozen. That means you can pull whatever amount you need from the freezer and have them baked and on the table in 30 minutes! Top with your favorite fresh Mexican toppings like guacamole, salsa, or sour cream and serve with a side salad for a satisfying meal that the whole family will love.

1 boneless beef chuck roast (about 3 pounds), trimmed of excess fat

3 tablespoons taco seasoning, homemade (see page 243) or store-bought

1 cup low-sodium beef broth

4 ounces cream cheese

½ cup mild or medium salsa

16 (8-inch) whole-wheat tortillas

About 3 cups shredded cheddar cheese

Cooking spray

Optional toppings: salsa, guacamole, sour cream or plain Greek yogurt

---

Slow Cooker • MAKES: 8 SERVINGS (2 TAQUITOS PER SERVING)

MAKE IT NOW

1   Place the roast in the slow cooker and rub the taco seasoning over all sides of the meat. Add the broth.

2   Cover and cook on Low for 8 to 10 hours or on High for 5 to 6 hours, until the meat easily shreds. Transfer the beef to a cutting board and discard the liquid in the cooker. Using two forks, shred the meat and return it to the cooker.

3   Add the cream cheese and salsa and stir until the cream cheese has melted.

4   Arrange the tortillas on a flat surface. Using a slotted spoon, top each tortilla with an equal amount of the beef mixture, leaving a little room at the edges so the filling doesn't spill out. Top each with about 3 tablespoons of the shredded cheese. Roll up the tortillas very tightly. *(Freezing instructions begin here.)*

(CONTINUES)

5   Preheat the oven to 400°F and position the racks in the upper and lower thirds. Spray two rimmed baking sheets with cooking spray or line them with parchment paper. (Alternatively, use one baking sheet to cook half the taquitos and freeze the rest to bake later.)

6   Arrange the taquitos seam-side down on the prepared baking sheets, squeezing them in side by side. Spray the tops with cooking spray and bake for 15 to 20 minutes, switching the pans from top to bottom halfway through the cooking time, until the cheese has melted and the tortillas are golden brown.

7   Serve warm, with your favorite toppings.

FREEZE FOR LATER: Follow steps 1 through 4. Place the rolled taquitos seam-side down in even layers (separated with parchment paper, if needed) in one or two gallon-size freezer bags or containers. Seal and freeze.

PREPARE FROM FROZEN: *Note: Have your favorite toppings on hand to complete this meal.* Two options:

1   Thaw. Follow steps 5 through 7.

2   Do not thaw. Follow steps 5 and 6, but cover the frozen taquitos with foil and bake for 25 minutes, then remove the foil and bake for 5 to 10 minutes more, until golden brown and completely warmed through. Follow step 7.

Instant Pot • MAKES: 8 SERVINGS (2 TAQUITOS PER SERVING)

MAKE IT NOW

1   Cut the beef into 2 × 2-inch pieces, trimming off excess fat as needed, and pat dry with paper towels. Place the beef in the 6-quart Instant Pot, sprinkle the taco seasoning over the beef, and toss to combine, coating all sides. Add the broth.

2   Lock and seal the lid. Cook at high pressure for 30 minutes. Allow the pressure to release naturally for 10 minutes, then quick release the remaining pressure. Use a slotted spoon to transfer the beef to a cutting board and discard the liquid in the pot. Using two forks, shred the meat and return it to the pot.

3   Add the cream cheese and salsa and stir until the cream cheese has melted.

4   Arrange the tortillas on a flat surface. Using a slotted spoon, top each tortilla with an equal amount of the beef mixture, leaving a little room at the edges so the filling doesn't spill out. Top each with about 3 tablespoons of the shredded cheese. Roll up the tortillas very tightly. *(Freezing instructions begin here.)*

5   Preheat the oven to 400°F and position the racks in the upper and lower thirds. Spray two rimmed baking sheets with cooking spray or line them with parchment paper. (Alternatively, use one baking sheet to cook half the taquitos and freeze the rest to bake later.)

6   Arrange the taquitos seam-side down on the prepared baking sheets, squeezing them in side by side. Spray the tops with cooking spray and bake for 15 to 20 minutes, switching the pans from top to bottom halfway through the cooking time, until the cheese has melted and the tortillas are golden brown.

7   Serve warm, with your favorite toppings.

FREEZE FOR LATER: Follow steps 1 through 4. Place the rolled taquitos seam-side down in even layers (separated with parchment paper, if needed) in one or two gallon-size freezer bags or containers. Seal and freeze.

PREPARE FROM FROZEN: *Note: Have your favorite toppings on hand to complete this meal.* Two options:

1   Thaw. Follow steps 5 through 7.

2   Do not thaw. Follow steps 5 and 6, but cover the frozen taquitos with foil and bake for 25 minutes, then remove the foil and bake for 5 to 10 minutes more, until golden brown and completely warmed through. Follow step 7.

Pulled Pork Mojo
Tacos, page 154

pork

BBQ PULLED PORK SANDWICHES

Who doesn't love a simple BBQ sandwich with moist shredded meat? That's why we've given you two options in this book—either using a beef roast (see page 110) or the pork shoulder here. Both cuts become fall-apart tender in either cooker. Our homemade BBQ sauce, made with ingredients you actually recognize (you can't say that about store brands!), is especially yummy over the meat.

1 teaspoon onion powder

1 teaspoon garlic powder

1 teaspoon salt

½ teaspoon ground black pepper

1 (3- to 4-pound) pork shoulder (also known as Boston butt), trimmed

1½ cups BBQ sauce, homemade (see page 236) or your favorite all-natural store-bought BBQ sauce

8 to 10 whole-wheat hamburger buns, toasted

Slow Cooker • MAKES: 8 TO 10 SERVINGS

MAKE IT NOW

1   In a small bowl, combine the onion powder, garlic powder, salt, and pepper.

2   Pat the pork shoulder dry with paper towels and rub it with the seasoning mix to coat all sides. *(Freezing instructions begin here.)*

3   Place the seasoned pork in the slow cooker and top with 1 cup of the BBQ sauce.

4   Cover and cook on Low for 7 to 9 hours or on High for 4 to 5 hours, until the meat easily shreds.

5   Transfer the pork to a cutting board and shred the meat. Return the meat to the slow cooker and stir it into the sauce.

6   Use a slotted spoon to transfer the meat to the toasted buns and top with the remaining BBQ sauce as desired. Serve.

FREEZE FOR LATER: Follow steps 1 and 2. Place the seasoned pork and 1 cup of the BBQ sauce in a gallon-size freezer bag or container. Seal and freeze. Place the remaining ½ cup BBQ sauce in a small freezer bag or container and the buns in a separate freezer bag. Seal and freeze them alongside the pork.

PREPARE FROM FROZEN: Thaw. Place the pork in the slow cooker. Follow steps 4 through 6.

(CONTINUES)

MAKE IT NOW

1   In a small bowl, combine the onion powder, garlic powder, salt, and pepper.

2   On a cutting board, cut the pork shoulder into four equal pieces. Pat the pork dry with paper towels and rub the pieces with the seasoning mix to coat all sides. *(Freezing instructions begin here.)*

3   Place the seasoned pork in the 6-quart Instant Pot. Pour 1 cup of the BBQ sauce over the meat and stir.

4   Lock and seal the lid. Cook at high pressure for 45 minutes. Allow the pressure to release naturally for 10 minutes (or longer, if you prefer), then quick release the remaining pressure.

5   Transfer the pork to a cutting board and shred the meat. Return the meat to the pot and stir it into the sauce.

6   Use a slotted spoon to transfer the meat to the toasted buns and top with the remaining BBQ sauce as desired. Serve.

FREEZE FOR LATER: Follow steps 1 and 2. Place the seasoned pork and 1 cup of the BBQ sauce in a gallon-size freezer bag or round container. Seal and freeze (if using a freezer bag, set it in a bowl or round container with a diameter similar to the Instant Pot so it will fit in the pot when frozen; see page 22). Place the remaining ½ cup BBQ sauce in a small freezer bag or container and the buns in a separate freezer bag. Seal and freeze them alongside the pork.

PREPARE FROM FROZEN: Thaw the sauce and buns. Set the Instant Pot to "Sauté." Transfer the frozen meal to the pot and cook for 5 minutes to release some liquid. Press "Cancel." Follow step 4, but cook at high pressure for 45 to 50 minutes. (The frozen meat will cook in about the same amount of time as fresh.) Follow steps 5 and 6.

MIX-AND-MATCH MEXICAN SHREDDED PORK

With a little kick of heat in the background and a note of chili flavor throughout, this versatile pulled pork can be used in so many ways. Change up taco night by using this filling instead of ground beef. Top a leafy green salad with it and other toppings like roasted fresh corn shaved off the cob, diced red bell peppers, red onion, and crunched-up tortilla chips. Throw this shredded pork in a quesadilla or on top of a "burrito bowl" with brown rice, beans, and your favorite Mexican toppings. So many possibilities! It's imperative to prep this a day ahead (or make it into a freezer meal) to make sure the rub has time to penetrate the roast before cooking.

Shortcut: *Wear disposable plastic gloves to make the prep and cleanup easier.*

1½ tablespoons chili powder

1 tablespoon ground cumin

1½ teaspoons salt

1½ teaspoons ground black pepper

¾ teaspoon garlic powder

¾ teaspoon onion powder

¾ teaspoon dried oregano

¾ teaspoon paprika

½ teaspoon cayenne pepper (or pull back to ¼ teaspoon for less spice)

3 tablespoons pure maple syrup

1 (3- to 4-pound) pork shoulder (also known as Boston butt), trimmed of excess fat

1 cup low-sodium chicken broth, homemade (see page 240) or store-bought (or substitute apple juice or water)

Slow Cooker • **MAKES: 8 TO 10 SERVINGS**

MAKE IT NOW

1   In a small bowl, use a fork to stir together the chili powder, cumin, salt, black pepper, garlic powder, onion powder, dried oregano, paprika, cayenne, and maple syrup to make a paste. Pat the pork shoulder dry with paper towels and, using the tip of a knife, poke several big slits in the meat on all sides. Using your hands, rub the paste all over the pork, working it down into the slits. *(Freezing instructions begin here.)*

2   Wrap the pork tightly in plastic wrap and refrigerate for 12 to 24 hours.

(CONTINUES)

3   Transfer the seasoned roast to the slow cooker and add the broth.

4   Cover and cook on Low for 7 to 9 hours or on High for 4 to 5 hours, until the meat shreds easily.

5   Transfer the pork to a cutting board and discard any liquid remaining in the cooker. Shred the meat, then return it to the slow cooker to keep it warm.

FREEZE FOR LATER: Follow step 1. Place the seasoned roast and the broth in a gallon-size freezer bag or container. Seal and freeze.

PREPARE FROM FROZEN: Thaw. Place in the slow cooker. Follow steps 4 through 5.

Instant Pot • MAKES: 8 TO 10 SERVINGS

MAKE IT NOW

1   In a small bowl, use a fork to stir together the chili powder, cumin, salt, black pepper, garlic powder, onion powder, dried oregano, paprika, cayenne, and maple syrup to make a paste.

2   On a cutting board, cut the pork shoulder into four equal pieces. Pat the pork dry with paper towels and rub the paste all over each piece. *(Freezing instructions begin here.)*

3   Wrap the pork tightly in plastic wrap and refrigerate for 12 to 24 hours.

4   Transfer the roast to the 6-quart Instant Pot and add the broth. Lock and seal the lid. Cook at high pressure for 45 minutes. Allow the pressure to release naturally for 10 minutes (or longer, if you prefer), then quick release the remaining pressure.

5   Transfer the pork to a cutting board and discard any liquid remaining in the pot. Use two forks to shred the meat, then return it to the pot to keep it warm.

FREEZE FOR LATER: Follow steps 1 and 2. Place the seasoned roast and broth in a gallon-size freezer bag or round container. Seal and freeze (if using a freezer bag, set it in a bowl or round container with a diameter similar to the Instant Pot so it will fit in the pot when frozen; see page 22).

PREPARE FROM FROZEN: Set the Instant Pot to "Sauté." Transfer the frozen meal to the pot and cook for 5 minutes to release some liquid. Press "Cancel." Follow step 4, but cook for 45 to 50 minutes. (The frozen meat will cook in about the same amount of time as fresh.) Follow step 5.

PULLED PORK MOJO TACOS

Contributed by Kristin Schell of The Turquoise Table

As a busy mama of four, I'm always on the lookout for quick and easy recipes that will satisfy my family's discerning taste buds. Years ago, a mojo-style pork recipe in a magazine caught my eye and inspired these tacos, which then became a slow cooker family favorite. Flavorful, adaptable, and deceptively simple, this delicious meal is perfect for a weeknight supper or a crowd-pleasing potluck. Adjust the seasonings to your heat tolerance. We like our tacos spicy in Texas, so I set out a bottle of Cholula for good measure. Bonus: The leftover pork is yummy on eggs for breakfast the next morning.

2 teaspoons salt

2 teaspoons dried oregano

2 teaspoons ground cumin

2 teaspoons paprika

2 teaspoons ground black pepper

¼ teaspoon cayenne pepper (optional, to add a kick of heat)

1 (3- to 4-pound) pork shoulder (also known as Boston butt), trimmed of excess fat

½ bunch fresh cilantro, chopped (about ½ cup; optional)

2 medium onions, halved and sliced

¼ cup canned chopped green chiles

4 garlic cloves, minced

2 cups low-sodium chicken broth, homemade (see page 240) or store-bought

⅔ cup freshly squeezed orange juice

½ cup freshly squeezed lime juice

8 to 10 (8-inch) whole-wheat or gluten-free tortillas

Optional toppings: shredded cheddar cheese,* sour cream,* sliced green onion, chopped fresh cilantro, chopped avocado, salsa, lime juice, etc.

Omit if making a dairy-free version.

Slow Cooker • MAKES: 8 TO 10 SERVINGS (2 TACOS PER SERVING)

MAKE IT NOW

1 In a small bowl, combine the salt, oregano, cumin, paprika, black pepper, and cayenne (if using).

2 Pat the pork shoulder dry with paper towels and rub the seasoning mixture over all sides of the pork. *(Freezing instructions begin here.)*

3 Place the pork in the slow cooker and top with the cilantro (if using), onions, chiles, garlic, broth, orange juice, and lime juice.

4 Cover and cook on Low for 7 to 9 hours or on High for 4 to 5 hours, until the meat easily shreds.

5   Transfer the pork to a cutting board. Using two forks, shred the pork and return it to the cooker.

6   Serve the pork on tortillas, with your favorite toppings.

FREEZE FOR LATER: Follow steps 1 and 2. Place the seasoned pork, cilantro (if using), onions, chiles, garlic, broth, orange juice, and lime juice in a gallon-size freezer bag or container. Seal, toss gently to combine, and freeze.

PREPARE FROM FROZEN: *Note: You will need to have tortillas and your choice of toppings on hand to complete this meal.* Thaw. Place in the slow cooker. Follow steps 4 through 6.

Instant Pot • MAKES: 8 TO 10 SERVINGS (2 TACOS PER SERVING)

MAKE IT NOW

1   In a small bowl, combine the salt, oregano, cumin, paprika, black pepper, and cayenne (if using).

2   Cut the pork shoulder into four equal pieces. Pat the pork dry with paper towels and rub the seasoning mixture over all sides of each piece. *(Freezing instructions begin here.)*

3   Place the pork in the 6-quart Instant Pot and top with the cilantro (if using), onions, chiles, garlic, broth, orange juice, and lime juice.

4   Lock and seal the lid. Cook at high pressure for 45 minutes. Allow the pressure to release naturally for 10 minutes (or longer, if you prefer), then quick release the remaining pressure.

5   Transfer the pork to a cutting board. Using two forks, shred the pork and return it to the pot.

6   Serve the pork on tortillas, with your favorite toppings.

FREEZE FOR LATER: Follow steps 1 and 2. Place the seasoned pork, cilantro (if using), onions, chiles, garlic, broth, orange juice, and lime juice in a gallon-size freezer bag or round container. Seal, toss gently to combine, and freeze.

PREPARE FROM FROZEN: *Note: You will need to have tortillas and your favorite toppings on hand to complete this meal.* Set the Instant Pot to "Sauté." Transfer the frozen meal to the pot and cook for 5 minutes to release some liquid. Press "Cancel." Follow step 4, but cook for 45 to 50 minutes. Follow steps 5 and 6.

BBQ BABY BACK RIBS

Cooking ribs is a breeze when you let your cooker do all the hard work. Our fall-off-the-bone-tender ribs are finished under the broiler to create a sticky glaze and caramelized edges. When ribs go on sale, stock up and make them into this freezer meal.

1 tablespoon salt	¼ teaspoon cayenne	1 to 2 cups BBQ sauce, homemade (see page 236) or your favorite all-natural store-bought BBQ sauce
2 teaspoons ground black pepper	2 tablespoons pure maple syrup	
2 teaspoons garlic powder	2 (2- to 2½-pound) racks pork baby back ribs, trimmed	
2 teaspoons paprika		

Slow Cooker • MAKES: 6 SERVINGS (4 OR 5 RIBS PER SERVING)

MAKE IT NOW

1   In a small bowl, use a fork to stir together the salt, black pepper, garlic powder, paprika, cayenne, and maple syrup to make a paste.

2   Pat the ribs dry with paper towels and rub the paste over all sides. *(Freezing instructions begin here.)*

3   Arrange the seasoned ribs standing on end around the perimeter of the cooker. The wider end should be at the bottom and the meaty side facing out. Cover and cook on Low for 5 to 7 hours, until the ribs are tender.

4   Position the top oven rack about 6 inches below the broiler. Preheat the broiler. Line a rimmed baking sheet with foil.

5   Using tongs, transfer the ribs to the prepared baking sheet, meaty-side down. Brush the ribs with some of the BBQ sauce on the top side. Broil for 2 to 4 minutes, until they start to brown. Flip, brush with more sauce, and broil for 6 to 10 minutes more, until well browned, brushing with sauce every few minutes.

6   Tent with foil and let rest for 10 minutes. Serve with the remaining BBQ sauce.

FREEZE FOR LATER: Follow steps 1 and 2. Place the seasoned ribs in one or two gallon-size freezer bags or containers. Seal and freeze. Place the BBQ sauce in a smaller freezer bag or container. Seal and freeze alongside the ribs.

PREPARE FROM FROZEN: Thaw. Follow steps 3 through 6.

(CONTINUES)

Instant Pot • MAKES: 6 SERVINGS (4 OR 5 RIBS PER SERVING)

Equipment Needed
Steamer rack/trivet with handles

MAKE IT NOW

1   In a small bowl, use a fork to stir together the salt, black pepper, garlic powder, paprika, cayenne, and maple syrup to make a paste.

2   Pat the ribs dry with paper towels, cut each rack in half (making four equal portions), and rub the paste over all sides. *(Freezing instructions begin here.)*

3   Pour 1 cup water into the 6-quart Instant Pot. Place a steamer rack in the pot and arrange the seasoned ribs on the rack, standing them on end in a tepee form. Lock and seal the lid. Cook at high pressure for 30 minutes, then quick release the pressure.

4   Position the top oven rack about 6 inches below the broiler. Preheat the broiler. Line a rimmed baking sheet with foil.

5   Using tongs, transfer the ribs to the prepared baking sheet, meaty-side down. Brush the ribs with some of the BBQ sauce on the top side. Broil for 2 to 4 minutes, until they start to brown. Flip, brush with more sauce, and broil for 6 to 10 minutes more, until well browned, brushing with sauce every few minutes.

6   Tent with foil and let rest for 10 minutes. Serve with the remaining BBQ sauce.

FREEZE FOR LATER: Follow steps 1 and 2. Place the seasoned ribs in one or two gallon-size freezer bags or round containers. Seal and freeze (if using a freezer bag, set it in a bowl or round container with a diameter similar to the Instant Pot so it will fit in the pot when frozen; see page 22). Place the BBQ sauce in a smaller freezer bag or container. Seal and freeze alongside the ribs.

PREPARE FROM FROZEN*: Thaw. Follow steps 3 through 6.

We have found that this recipe cooks unevenly from frozen in the Instant Pot. Because of this, we recommend thawing and cooking from fresh for best results.

MAPLE-GLAZED PORK LOIN

The combination of maple syrup, soy sauce, and fresh ginger in this recipe adds a delicious sweet-savory combo to the pork. Since a pork loin roast (not to be confused with its close cousin, the pork tenderloin, or a pork shoulder) can easily dry out, make sure to take an internal temperature and stop cooking it when it reaches 145°F. It will still be slightly pink on the inside when done.

1 (2½- to 3-pound) boneless pork loin roast, trimmed of excess fat

Salt and ground black pepper

1 tablespoon avocado oil or olive oil

½ onion, diced

2 garlic cloves, minced

⅓ cup low-sodium soy sauce

⅔ cup pure maple syrup

1 tablespoon chopped fresh ginger

⅛ teaspoon cayenne pepper

2 tablespoons cornstarch

Slow Cooker • MAKES: 6 TO 8 SERVINGS

MAKE IT NOW

1   Pat the pork dry with paper towels, season it lightly on all sides with salt and black pepper, and place in a gallon-size freezer bag or container with a lid.

2   In a medium skillet, heat the oil over medium-high heat until shimmery. Add the onion and cook, stirring, until just beginning to soften, 4 to 5 minutes. Stir in the garlic during the last 30 to 60 seconds of cooking. Remove from the heat.

3   Transfer the onion mixture to the bag/container with the pork and add the soy sauce, maple syrup, ginger, and cayenne. Seal tightly and toss to combine. *(Freezing instructions begin here.)*

4   Marinate the pork in the refrigerator for at least 2 hours and up to 24 hours.

5   Transfer the pork and marinade to the slow cooker. Cover and cook on Low for 3 to 4 hours. (The pork is done when it registers 145°F internally.)

6   Transfer the pork to a cutting board, tent with foil, and let rest for about 10 minutes.

7   Carefully pour or ladle the juices from the slow cooker into a medium saucepan. In a small bowl, stir together the cornstarch and 2 tablespoons

(CONTINUES)

water until smooth. Add the cornstarch mixture to the pan and bring to a boil over high heat. Reduce the heat to maintain a simmer and cook, whisking, until thickened, about 3 minutes. Remove from the heat. Taste and season with salt and black pepper, if desired.

8   Cut the pork into ½-inch-thick slices. Fan them out on a serving platter and drizzle the sauce over the meat. Serve.

FREEZE FOR LATER: Follow steps 1 through 3. Freeze the pork and marinade.

PREPARE FROM FROZEN: *Note: You will need to have cornstarch, salt, and pepper on hand to complete the meal.* Thaw. Follow steps 5 through 8.

Instant Pot • MAKES: 6 TO 8 SERVINGS

MAKE IT NOW

1   Pat the pork dry with paper towels, season it lightly on all sides with salt and black pepper, and place in a gallon-size freezer bag.

2   Set the 6-quart Instant Pot to "Sauté." Pour the oil into the pot and heat until shimmery. Add the onion and cook, stirring, until just beginning to soften, 4 o 5 minutes. Stir in the garlic during the last 30 to 60 seconds of cooking. Press "Cancel."

3   Transfer the onion mixture to the bag/container with the pork and add the soy sauce, maple syrup, ginger, and cayenne. Seal tightly and toss to combine. *(Freezing instructions begin here.)*

4   Marinate the pork in the refrigerator for at least 2 hours and up to 24 hours.

5   Transfer the pork and marinade to the Instant Pot.

6   Lock and seal the lid. Cook at high pressure for 27 minutes, then allow the pressure to release naturally, about 10 minutes. Transfer the pork to a cutting board, tent with foil, and let rest for about 10 minutes.

7   Set the Instant Pot to "Sauté." In a small bowl, stir together the cornstarch and 2 tablespoons water until smooth. Stir the cornstarch mixture into the sauce remaining in the pot and bring to a boil. Cook, whisking, until thickened, about 3 minutes. Press "Cancel." Taste and season with salt and black pepper, if desired.

8   Cut the pork into ½-inch-thick slices. Fan them out on a serving platter and drizzle the sauce over the meat. Serve.

FREEZE FOR LATER: Cut the pork loin into three equal pieces. Follow steps 1 through 3. Freeze the pork and marinade.

PREPARE FROM FROZEN: *Note: You will need to have cornstarch, salt, pepper, and (optional) cooked rice on hand to complete this meal.* Set the Instant Pot to "Sauté." Transfer the frozen meal to the pot and cook for 5 minutes to release some liquid. Press "Cancel." Follow steps 6 through 8. (The frozen meat will cook in about the same amount of time as fresh.)

GREEK PULLED PORK PITAS

Both picky and adventurous eaters will go for this Mediterranean spin on pulled pork. Serve the meat wrapped in soft, whole-wheat pita bread topped with chopped fresh veggies, tangy feta cheese, and our creamy, herb-infused tzatziki sauce. (It's worth noting that this sauce tastes even better after sitting in the fridge for a day.) If your people are picky (like some unnamed small ones in our homes), they'll still love the pulled pork just wrapped by itself in a warm pita.

Recipe Testing Team Tip: *"I ended up mixing the pork, sauce, tomatoes, olives, and feta in a bowl first and then spooning the mixture into the warm pita. This made sure each bite was a yummy mixture of flavors."* —Jen G.

Pork Filling

1½ teaspoons dried oregano

1½ teaspoons ground cumin

1 teaspoon salt

1½ teaspoons ground black pepper

¼ teaspoon red pepper flakes

5 or 6 garlic cloves, minced

1 (3- to 4-pound) pork shoulder (also known as Boston butt), trimmed of excess fat

1 red onion, thinly sliced

1 cup low-sodium chicken broth, homemade (see page 240) or store-bought

Pita and Toppings

8 to 10 pocketless pita breads (preferably whole wheat)

Tzatziki Sauce (recipe follows)

Optional toppings: chopped cherry tomatoes, sliced cucumbers, chopped kalamata olives, shredded cabbage or lettuce, crumbled feta cheese

---

Slow Cooker • MAKES: 8 TO 10 SERVINGS

MAKE IT NOW

1 *For the pork filling:* In a small bowl, combine the oregano, cumin, salt, black pepper, red pepper flakes, and garlic.

2 Pat the pork shoulder dry with paper towels. Rub the seasoning mixture over the pork on all sides. *(Freezing instructions begin here.)*

3 Place the pork, onion, and broth in the slow cooker. Cover and cook on Low for 7 to 9 hours or on High for 4 to 5 hours.

4 Transfer the pork and onion to a cutting board and discard any liquid remaining in the cooker. Shred the meat, then return the meat and the onion to the pot to keep it warm.

(CONTINUES)

5   Serve the shredded pork wrapped in a warm pita bread, topped with the tzatziki and your favorite Greek toppings.

FREEZE FOR LATER: Follow steps 1 and 2. Place the pork, onion, and broth in a gallon-size freezer bag or container. Seal and freeze. Freeze the pita bread alongside the pork.

PREPARE FROM FROZEN: *Note: You will need to have Tzatziki Sauce and your favorite toppings on hand to complete this meal.* Thaw. Follow steps 3 through 5.

Instant Pot • MAKES: 8 TO 10 SERVINGS

MAKE IT NOW

1   *For the pork filling:* In a small bowl, combine the oregano, cumin, salt, black pepper, red pepper flakes, and garlic.

2   On a cutting board, cut the pork shoulder into four equal pieces. Pat the pork dry with paper towels and rub the seasoning mix all over each piece. *(Freezing instructions begin here.)*

3   Place the pork, onion, and broth in the 6-quart Instant Pot.

4   Lock and seal the lid. Cook at high pressure for 45 minutes. Allow the pressure to release naturally for 10 minutes, then quick release the remaining pressure.

5   Transfer the pork and onion to a cutting board and discard any liquid remaining in the pot. Using two forks, shred the meat, then return the meat and onion to the pot to keep warm.

6   Serve the shredded pork wrapped in a warm pita bread, topped with the tzatziki and your favorite Greek toppings.

FREEZE FOR LATER: Follow steps 1 and 2. Place the seasoned pork, onion, and broth in a gallon-size freezer bag or round container. Seal and freeze. Freeze the pita bread alongside the pork.

PREPARE FROM FROZEN: *Note: You will need to have Tzatziki Sauce and your favorite toppings on hand to complete this meal.* Set the Instant Pot to "Sauté." Transfer the frozen meal to the pot and cook for 5 minutes to release some liquid. Press "Cancel." Follow step 4, but cook for 45 to 50 minutes. (The frozen meat will cook in about the same amount of time as fresh.) Follow steps 5 and 6.

TZATZIKI SAUCE
MAKES: ABOUT 1½ CUPS

1 cup plain full-fat Greek yogurt

½ cup finely diced or shredded peeled seedless cucumber

1 tablespoon minced fresh mint

1 tablespoon minced fresh dill, or 1 teaspoon dried

1 tablespoon fresh lemon juice (about ½ small lemon)

1 tablespoon extra-virgin olive oil

2 garlic cloves, minced

Salt and ground black pepper

In a medium bowl, stir together the yogurt, cucumber, mint, dill, lemon juice, olive oil, and garlic until creamy and well combined. Taste and season with salt and pepper. Cover and refrigerate until ready to use, up to 3 days. (Do not freeze this sauce.)

CUBAN-STYLE PORK PANINIS

These paninis were a surprise favorite among our family and friends. The pork absorbs the flavors of the citrus-infused marinade and practically falls apart after cooking. The mustard, pickles, and Swiss cheese bring a punch of flavor, a little crunch, and some gooey goodness, respectively. All these ingredients together make for one amazing hot sandwich.

2 tablespoons avocado oil or olive oil

Zest and juice of 1 lime

Zest and juice of 1 orange

3 garlic cloves, minced

2 teaspoons dried oregano

2 teaspoons ground cumin

¼ teaspoon red pepper flakes

2 teaspoons salt

1 teaspoon ground black pepper

1 (3- to 4-pound) pork shoulder (also known as Boston butt), trimmed of excess fat

1 cup low-sodium chicken broth, homemade (see page 240) or store-bought (for Instant Pot only)

About ½ cup (1 stick) butter, at room temperature

8 to 10 whole-wheat ciabatta rolls, sliced open

Yellow mustard

8 to 10 thick slices Swiss cheese

1 pound thinly sliced honey ham

2 cups all-natural dill pickle chips or sandwich slices

Slow Cooker • MAKES: 8 TO 10 SERVINGS

MAKE IT NOW

1   In a small bowl, combine the oil, lime zest, lime juice, orange zest, orange juice, garlic, oregano, cumin, red pepper flakes, salt, and black pepper.

2   Pat the pork dry with paper towels and rub the seasoning mixture over all sides. *(Freezing instructions begin here.)*

3   Place the pork in the slow cooker. Cover and cook on Low for 7 to 9 hours or on High for 4 to 5 hours, until the meat easily shreds.

4   Transfer the pork to a cutting board and use two forks to shred the meat. Return the meat to the slow cooker and keep warm in the cooking liquid.

5   Spread a thin layer of butter over the outside of each ciabatta. Open them up and smear the insides with mustard on both sides. Layer 1 slice of Swiss, a couple of pieces of ham, some warm pulled pork (use a slotted spoon to remove it from the cooking liquid), and a layer of pickles.

(CONTINUES)

6   Heat a large skillet or griddle over medium heat. Grill the sandwiches for a few minutes on each side, pressing down on them with a spatula or a heavy pan as they cook, until the bread is golden brown on both sides and the cheese has melted. Serve warm.

FREEZE FOR LATER: Follow steps 1 and 2. Place the seasoned pork shoulder in a gallon-size freezer bag or container. Seal and freeze. Place the ciabatta rolls, cheese, and ham in separate freezer bags or containers. Seal and freeze alongside the pork.

PREPARE FROM FROZEN: *Note: You will need to have butter, mustard, and pickles on hand to complete this meal.* Thaw. Follow steps 3 through 6.

Instant Pot • MAKES: 8 TO 10 SERVINGS

MAKE IT NOW

1   In a small bowl, combine the oil, lime zest, lime juice, orange zest, orange juice, garlic, oregano, cumin, red pepper flakes, salt, and black pepper.

2   Cut the pork into four equal pieces. Pat the pork dry with paper towels and rub the seasoning mixture over all sides of each piece. *(Freezing instructions begin here.)*

3   Place the pork in the 6-quart Instant Pot and add the broth.

4   Lock and seal the lid. Cook at high pressure for 45 minutes. Allow the pressure to release naturally for 10 minutes (or longer, if you prefer), then quick release the remaining pressure.

5   Transfer the pork to a cutting board and use two forks to shred the meat. Return the meat to the Instant Pot and keep warm in the cooking liquid.

6   Spread a thin layer of butter over the outside of each ciabatta. Open them up and smear the insides with mustard on both sides. Layer 1 slice of Swiss, a couple of pieces of ham, some warm pulled pork (use a slotted spoon to remove it from the cooking liquid), and a layer of pickles.

7   Heat a large skillet or griddle over medium heat. Grill the sandwiches for a few minutes on each side, pressing down on them with a spatula or a heavy pan as they cook, until the bread is golden brown on both sides and the cheese has melted. Serve warm.

FREEZE FOR LATER: Follow steps 1 and 2. Place the seasoned pork shoulder and the broth in a gallon-size freezer bag or container. Seal and freeze (if using a freezer bag, set it in a bowl or round container with a diameter similar to the Instant Pot so it will fit in the pot when frozen; see page 22). Place the ciabatta rolls, cheese, and ham in separate freezer bags or containers. Seal and freeze alongside the pork.

PREPARE FROM FROZEN: *Note: You will need to have butter, mustard, and pickles on hand to complete this meal.* Thaw the ciabatta rolls, cheese, and ham. Set the Instant Pot to "Sauté." Transfer the frozen pork to the pot and cook for 5 minutes to release some liquid. Press "Cancel." Follow steps 3 through 6. (The frozen meat will cook in about the same amount of time as fresh.)

Creamy Tomato
Basil Soup, *page 172*

soups, chilis & stews

CREAMY TOMATO BASIL SOUP

This simple, creamy, slightly sweet tomato soup works every time. Pair it with its life partner, grilled cheese, and you'll have a cheap, healthy dinner on the table with minimal effort. The fire-roasted tomatoes and fresh basil turn what could be a bland soup into something complex.

1 tablespoon avocado oil or olive oil

1 medium yellow onion, diced (about 1 cup)

2 or 3 carrots, diced (about 1 cup)

⅛ teaspoon red pepper flakes

Salt and ground black pepper

2 garlic cloves, minced

2 cups low-sodium vegetable broth or chicken broth, homemade (see page 240) or store-bought

2 (14.5-ounce) cans fire-roasted diced tomatoes, with their juices

3 tablespoons tomato paste

2 teaspoons sugar

¼ cup packed chopped fresh basil leaves

2 tablespoons butter

½ cup half-and-half, or more to taste

Freshly grated Parmesan cheese, for serving

Slow Cooker • MAKES: 4 OR 5 SERVINGS

MAKE IT NOW

1   In a large skillet, heat the oil over medium-high heat until shimmery. Add the onion and carrots and cook, stirring, until just beginning to soften, about 4 minutes, seasoning with the red pepper flakes and lightly with salt and black pepper as they cook. Stir in the garlic during the last 30 to 60 seconds of cooking. *(Freezing instructions begin here.)*

2   Transfer the veggie mixture to the slow cooker. Add the broth, tomatoes, tomato paste, and sugar. Season lightly with more salt and black pepper and stir to combine.

3   Cover and cook on Low for 4 to 6 hours.

4   Stir the basil into the soup. Using an immersion blender, puree the soup directly in the slow cooker until very smooth. Alternatively, carefully transfer the soup to a blender, working in batches as needed, and puree until very smooth. Return the soup to the slow cooker.

5   Add the butter and half-and-half to the soup and stir until the butter has melted. Taste and season with salt and black pepper.

6   Ladle the soup into bowls and top with freshly shredded Parmesan to serve.

FREEZE FOR LATER: Follow step 1. Let the veggie mixture cool, then transfer it to a gallon-size freezer bag or container. Add the broth, tomatoes, tomato paste, and sugar. Season lightly with salt and black pepper. Seal, toss to combine, and freeze.

PREPARE FROM FROZEN: *Note: You will need to have basil, butter, half-and-half, salt, pepper, and Parmesan on hand to complete this meal.* Thaw. Place in the slow cooker. Follow steps 3 through 6.

Instant Pot • MAKES: 4 OR 5 SERVINGS

MAKE IT NOW

1   Set the 6-quart Instant Pot to "Sauté." Pour the oil into the pot and heat until shimmery. Add the onion and carrots and cook, stirring, until just beginning to soften, about 4 minutes. Season with the red pepper flakes and lightly with salt and black pepper as they cook and stir in the garlic during the last 30 to 60 seconds of cooking. Press "Cancel."

2   Add the broth, tomatoes, tomato paste, and sugar. Season lightly with more salt and black pepper and stir to combine. *(Freezing instructions begin here.)*

3   Lock and seal the lid. Cook at high pressure for 7 minutes, then quick release the pressure.

4   Stir the basil into the soup. Using an immersion blender, puree the soup directly in the pot until very smooth. Alternatively, carefully transfer the soup to a blender, working in batches as needed, and puree until very smooth. Return the soup to the Instant Pot.

5   Add the butter and half-and-half to the soup and stir until the butter has melted. Taste and season with salt and black pepper.

6   Ladle the soup into bowls and top with freshly shredded Parmesan to serve.

FREEZE FOR LATER: Follow steps 1 and 2. Let the soup cool, then carefully transfer the uncooked soup to a gallon-size freezer bag or round container (see p. 22 for freezing tips). Seal and freeze.

PREPARE FROM FROZEN: *Note: You will need to have basil, butter, half-and-half, salt, pepper, and Parmesan on hand to complete this meal.* Set the Instant Pot to "Sauté." Transfer the frozen soup to the pot and cook for 5 minutes to release some liquid. Press "Cancel." Follow step 3, but cook for 12 to 15 minutes. Follow steps 4 through 6.

CHICKEN TACO SOUP

Take this big-batch soup along to tailgate parties or freeze in small portions for future healthy lunches. It's got a nice little spicy kick that adults love. For heat-sensitive palates, though, we suggest cutting the taco seasoning in half.

1 to 2 tablespoons avocado oil or olive oil

1 onion, diced (about 1 cup)

2 bell peppers (we recommend one red and one green), diced

Salt and ground black pepper

3 garlic cloves, minced

1½ pounds boneless, skinless medium chicken breasts

1 (28-ounce) can petite diced tomatoes (or two 14.5-ounce cans), with their juices

1 (15-ounce) can black beans, drained and rinsed

1 (15-ounce) can pinto beans, drained and rinsed

1 (15-ounce) can corn, drained and rinsed

1 cup mild salsa

3 cups (for slow cooker) or 2 cups (for Instant Pot) low-sodium chicken broth, homemade (see page 240) or store-bought

3 tablespoons taco seasoning, homemade (see page 243) or store-bought

Optional toppings: sliced avocado, lime wedges, sour cream or plain Greek yogurt,* shredded cheddar cheese,* sliced green onions, corn tortilla chips, hot sauce

*Omit if making a dairy-free version.

Slow Cooker • MAKES: 8 TO 10 SERVINGS

MAKE IT NOW

1   In a large skillet, heat the oil over medium-high heat until shimmery. Add the onion and bell peppers and cook until they begin to soften, about 5 minutes, seasoning lightly with salt and black pepper while they cook. Stir in the garlic during the last 30 to 60 seconds of cooking. *(Freezing instructions begin here.)*

2   Transfer the veggie mixture to the cooker and add the chicken, tomatoes, black beans, pinto beans, corn, salsa, broth, and taco seasoning. Stir to combine.

3   Cover and cook on Low for 4 to 6 hours, until the chicken is cooked through. (The chicken is done when it is no longer pink inside and/or registers 165°F internally.)

4   Transfer the chicken to a cutting board and shred with two forks or chop into bite-size pieces. Return the chicken to the cooker and stir it into the soup.

5   Taste and season with salt and black pepper. Serve warm, topped with your favorite toppings.

(CONTINUES)

FREEZE FOR LATER: Follow step 1. Let the veggies cool, then transfer them to one or two gallon-size freezer bags or containers and add the chicken, tomatoes, black beans, pinto beans, corn, salsa, broth, and taco seasoning. Seal and freeze.

PREPARE FROM FROZEN: *Note: Have salt, pepper, and your favorite toppings on hand to complete this meal.* Thaw. Place in the slow cooker. Follow steps 3 through 5.

Instant Pot • MAKES: 8 TO 10 SERVINGS

MAKE IT NOW

1   Set the 6-quart Instant Pot to "Sauté." Pour the oil into the pot and heat until shimmery. Add the onion and bell peppers and cook until they begin to soften, 5 to 7 minutes, seasoning lightly with salt and pepper while they cook. Stir in the garlic during the last 30 to 60 seconds of cooking. Press "Cancel." *(Freezing instructions begin here.)*

2   Add the chicken, tomatoes, black beans, pinto beans, corn, salsa, broth, and taco seasoning to the Instant Pot. Stir to combine.

3   Lock and seal the lid. Cook at high pressure for 6 minutes, then quick release the pressure. (The chicken is done when it is no longer pink inside and/or registers 165°F internally.)

4   Transfer the chicken to a cutting board and shred with two forks or chop into bite-size pieces. Return the chicken to the pot and stir it into the soup.

5   Taste and season with salt and black pepper. Serve warm, topped with your favorite toppings.

FREEZE FOR LATER: Follow step 1. Let the veggies cool, then transfer them to one or two gallon-size freezer bags or round containers and add the chicken, tomatoes, black beans, pinto beans, corn, salsa, broth, and taco seasoning (try not to stack the chicken breasts in the bag/container; instead, place them side by side). Seal and freeze (if using a freezer bag, set it in a bowl or round container with a diameter similar to the Instant Pot so it will fit in the pot when frozen; see page 22).

PREPARE FROM FROZEN: *Note: Have salt, pepper, and your favorite toppings on hand to complete this meal.* Set the Instant Pot to "Sauté." Transfer the frozen meal to the pot and cook for 5 to 10 minutes to release some liquid. Press "Cancel." Follow step 3, but cook for 22 to 27 minutes. Follow steps 4 and 5.

LOADED CHEDDAR POTATO SOUP

This veggie-rich soup is perfect on a cool fall evening or cold winter's night. We will go on record that the half-and-half makes this soup what it is. It just wasn't the same when we tested it with milk. Oh, and don't forget the crumbled bacon at the end. Just go for it.

Shortcut: *To save time, use unpeeled baby Yukon Gold potatoes. They don't require peeling, saving you on the prep time.*

4 to 6 slices uncured bacon

1¼ cups diced onion (about 1 onion)

1 cup diced celery (2 to 3 stalks)

1 cup diced carrots (2 to 3 carrots)

Salt and ground black pepper

2 garlic cloves, minced

3 cups low-sodium chicken broth, homemade (see page 240) or store-bought

½ teaspoon paprika

¼ teaspoon dried thyme

3 cups ½-inch-diced peeled russet potatoes (about 3 medium)

1 cup half-and-half

2 cups grated medium or sharp cheddar cheese

Minced fresh chives or sliced green onions, for serving

Slow Cooker • MAKES: 4 TO 6 SERVINGS

MAKE IT NOW

1   In a large skillet, fry the bacon over medium-high heat until crisp on both sides. Transfer to a paper towel–lined plate, leaving the bacon grease in the pan. Crumble the bacon and set aside in the refrigerator.

2   Return the pan to medium-high heat. Add the onion, celery, and carrots and cook until tender, about 5 minutes. Lightly season them with salt and pepper as they cook and stir in the garlic during the last 30 to 60 seconds of cooking. *(Freezing instructions begin here.)*

3   Transfer the veggies to the slow cooker and add the broth, paprika, thyme, potatoes, 1 teaspoon salt, and ½ teaspoon pepper. Stir to combine.

4   Cover and cook on Low for about 8 hours, or until the potatoes are very tender.

5   If desired, use a potato masher to mash the potatoes to your preferred texture.

6   Stir in the half-and-half. Slowly add the cheese, stirring it in a little at a time until it's melted and well combined. Taste and season with salt and pepper.

7   Serve bowls of the soup topped with the bacon and chives or green onions.

(CONTINUES)

FREEZE FOR LATER: Follow steps 1 and 2. Let the veggies cool, then transfer them to a gallon-size freezer bag or container and add the broth, paprika, thyme, potatoes, 1 teaspoon salt, and ½ teaspoon pepper. Seal, making sure the potatoes are completely submerged in the liquid to prevent browning, and freeze. Place the bacon and cheese in separate freezer bags. Seal and freeze alongside the soup.

PREPARE FROM FROZEN: *Note: Have half-and-half and chives on hand to complete this meal.* Thaw. Place in the slow cooker. Follow steps 4 through 7.

Instant Pot • MAKES: 4 TO 6 SERVINGS

MAKE IT NOW

1   Place the bacon in the 6-quart Instant Pot, then set the pot to "Sauté." Fry the bacon until crisp on both sides. Transfer to a paper towel–lined plate, leaving the bacon grease in the pot. Crumble the bacon and set aside in the refrigerator.

2   Add the onion, celery, and carrots to the pot and cook, stirring, until tender, 4 to 5 minutes. Lightly season them with salt and pepper as they cook and stir in the garlic during the last 30 to 60 seconds of cooking. Press "Cancel."

3   Stir in the broth, paprika, thyme, potatoes, 1 teaspoon salt, and ½ teaspoon pepper. *(Freezing instructions begin here.)*

4   Lock and seal the lid. Cook at high pressure for 7 minutes, then quick release the pressure.

5   If desired, use a potato masher to mash the potatoes to your preferred texture.

6   Stir in the half-and-half. Slowly add the cheese, stirring it in a little at a time until it's melted and well combined. Taste and season with salt and pepper.

7   Serve bowls of the soup topped with the bacon and chives or green onions.

FREEZE FOR LATER: Follow steps 1 through 3. Transfer the uncooked soup to a gallon-size freezer bag or round container. Seal, making sure the potatoes are completely submerged in the liquid to prevent browning, and freeze. Place the bacon and cheese in separate freezer bags. Seal and freeze alongside the soup.

PREPARE FROM FROZEN: *Note: You will need half-and-half and chives on hand to complete this meal.* Thaw the bacon and cheese. Set the Instant Pot to "Sauté." Transfer the frozen soup to the pot and cook for 5 minutes. Press "Cancel." Follow step 4, but cook for 12 to 17 minutes. Follow steps 5 through 7.

LEMONY CHICKEN SOUP
WITH ORZO

Spring comes to mind when we make this soup, because it's light and fresh, and has pops of green. The fresh lemon juice brings a citrusy dimension that takes the flavor beyond your typical chicken noodle soup. But if lemon isn't your thing, just leave it out. Orzo is a fun little pasta shaped like rice that pairs well with the chicken and veggies. Once the orzo is added, serve the soup immediately, as the pasta will suck up the liquid quickly. If rewarming the next day, add more broth as needed.

Recipe Testing Team Tip: *Substitute great northern beans for the chicken if you want a meatless meal.*

1 to 2 tablespoons avocado oil or olive oil

1 cup diced onion

2 cups diced carrots

Salt and ground black pepper

3 garlic cloves, minced

½ teaspoon dried Italian seasoning

1 pound boneless, skinless medium chicken breasts

6 cups low-sodium chicken broth, homemade (see page 240) or store-bought

2 bay leaves

¾ cup uncooked orzo

2 cups packed baby spinach, coarsely chopped

Juice of 1 large lemon

Shredded Parmesan cheese,* for serving (optional)

*Omit if making a dairy-free version.

Slow Cooker • MAKES: 4 SERVINGS

MAKE IT NOW

1   In a large skillet, heat the oil over medium-high heat until shimmery. Add the onion and carrots and cook, stirring, until softened, 4 to 5 minutes. Season lightly with salt and pepper while they cook and stir in the garlic and Italian seasoning during the last 30 to 60 seconds of cooking. *(Freezing instructions begin here.)*

2   Transfer the veggie mixture to the slow cooker. Place the chicken on top and season on all sides with ¼ teaspoon salt and ¼ teaspoon pepper. Stir in the broth and bay leaves.

(CONTINUES)

3   Cover and cook on Low for 3 to 4 hours, until the chicken is cooked through. (The chicken is done when it is no longer pink inside and/or registers 165°F internally.) Transfer the chicken to a cutting board and set aside.

4   Set the slow cooker to High. Quickly stir in the orzo, cover, and cook for 20 to 30 minutes more, until the orzo is just al dente. (Do not overcook.) Meanwhile, shred or chop the chicken into bite-size pieces.

5   Discard the bay leaves and stir in the chicken, spinach, and lemon juice. Taste and season with salt and pepper.

6   Serve immediately, topped with shredded Parmesan, if desired.

FREEZE FOR LATER: Follow step 1. Let the veggie mixture cool, then transfer it to a gallon-size freezer bag or container. Season the chicken on all sides with ¼ teaspoon salt and ¼ teaspoon pepper. Add the chicken, broth, and bay leaves to the bag/container. Seal and freeze.

PREPARE FROM FROZEN: *Note: You will need to have orzo, spinach, lemon juice, salt, pepper, and (optional) Parmesan on hand to complete this meal.* Thaw. Pour the soup into the slow cooker and follow steps 3 through 6.

Instant Pot • MAKES: 4 SERVINGS

MAKE IT NOW

1   Set the 6-quart Instant Pot to "Sauté." Pour the oil into the pot and heat until shimmery. Add the onion and carrots and cook, stirring, until softened, 4 to 5 minutes, seasoning lightly with salt and pepper while they cook and stirring in the garlic and Italian seasoning during the last 30 to 60 seconds of cooking. Press "Cancel." *(Freezing instructions begin here.)*

2   Season the chicken on both sides with ¼ teaspoon salt and ¼ teaspoon pepper and add it to the pot. Stir in the broth and bay leaves.

3   Lock and seal the lid. Cook at high pressure for 6 minutes, then quick release the pressure. (The chicken is done when it is no longer pink inside and/or registers 165°F internally.) Transfer the chicken to a cutting board.

4   Set the Instant Pot to "Sauté." Stir in the orzo and cook for a few minutes less than directed on the package, until just al dente. Meanwhile, shred or chop the chicken into bite-size pieces.

5   Press "Cancel." Discard the bay leaves and stir in the chicken, spinach, and lemon juice. Taste and season with salt and pepper.

6   Serve immediately, topped with shredded Parmesan, if desired.

FREEZE FOR LATER: Follow step 1. Let the veggie mixture cool, then transfer it to a gallon-size freezer bag or round container. Season the chicken on all sides with ¼ teaspoon salt and ¼ teaspoon pepper. Add the chicken, broth, and bay leaves to the bag/container (do not stack the chicken breasts in the bag/container; instead, place them side by side). Seal and freeze (if using a freezer bag, set it in a bowl or round container with a diameter similar to the Instant Pot so it will fit in the pot when frozen; see page 22).

PREPARE FROM FROZEN: *Note: You will need to have orzo, spinach, lemon juice, salt, pepper, and (optional) Parmesan on hand to complete this meal.* Set the Instant Pot to "Sauté." Transfer the frozen soup to the pot and cook for 5 minutes to release some liquid. Press "Cancel." Follow step 3, but cook for 17 to 22 minutes. Follow steps 4 through 6.

PIZZA SOUP

Two of our favorite foods—pizza and soup—come together in this gluten-free, dairy-free recipe to create a meal that's healthy, filling, and incredibly tasty. Pizza Soup was inspired by Joanne, one of our most loyal recipe testers; she makes a similar one for her children, who have food allergies. At the store, look for all-natural chicken sausage and uncured pepperoni.

1 tablespoon avocado oil or olive oil

12 ounces fully cooked mild Italian chicken sausage, halved and sliced into half moons

1 onion, diced (about 1 cup)

Pinch of red pepper flakes

2 garlic cloves, minced

1 (24-ounce) jar marinara sauce, or 3 cups homemade marinara sauce (see page 216)

1 (14.5-ounce) can fire-roasted diced tomatoes, with their juices

2 cups low-sodium chicken broth, homemade (see page 240) or store-bought

4 ounces uncured turkey pepperoni (we recommend Applegate), quartered

1 medium zucchini, diced (about 2 cups)

8 ounces button mushrooms, chopped (2 to 3 cups)

1 teaspoon dried oregano

2 cups chopped baby spinach

Slow Cooker • **MAKES: 6 SERVINGS**

MAKE IT NOW

1   In a medium skillet, heat the oil over medium-high heat until shimmery. Add the sausage and cook, stirring, for 4 to 5 minutes, until browned. Transfer the sausage to the slow cooker.

2   Add the onion to the skillet and cook, stirring, until softened, about 4 minutes, stirring in the red pepper flakes and garlic during the last 30 to 60 seconds of cooking. *(Freezing instructions begin here.)*

3   Transfer the onion mixture to the slow cooker and add the marinara, tomatoes, broth, pepperoni, zucchini, mushrooms, oregano, and spinach. Stir to combine.

4   Cover and cook on Low for 6 to 8 hours. Serve.

(CONTINUES)

FREEZE FOR LATER: Follow step 1, but transfer the sausage to a plate to cool. Follow step 2. Let the onion cool, then transfer the sausage and the onion to a gallon-size freezer bag or container and add the marinara, tomatoes, broth, pepperoni, zucchini, mushrooms, oregano, and spinach. Seal, toss gently to combine, and freeze.

PREPARE FROM FROZEN: Thaw. Transfer the soup to the slow cooker and follow step 4.

Instant Pot • MAKES: 6 SERVINGS

MAKE IT NOW

1   Set the 6-quart Instant Pot to "Sauté." Pour the oil into the pot and heat until shimmery. Add the sausage and cook, stirring, for 4 to 5 minutes, until browned. Set aside on a plate.

2   Add the onion to the pot and cook, stirring, until softened, about 4 minutes, stirring in the red pepper flakes and garlic during the last 30 to 60 seconds of cooking. Press "Cancel."

3   Stir in the sausage, marinara, tomatoes, broth, pepperoni, zucchini, mushrooms, oregano, and spinach. *(Freezing instructions begin here.)*

4   Lock and seal the lid. Cook at high pressure for 7 minutes, then quick release the pressure. Serve.

FREEZE FOR LATER: Follow steps 1 through 3. Carefully transfer the uncooked soup to a gallon-size freezer bag or round container. Seal and freeze (if using a freezer bag, set it in a bowl or round container with a diameter similar to the Instant Pot so it will fit in the pot when frozen; see page 22).

PREPARE FROM FROZEN: Set the Instant Pot to "Sauté." Transfer the frozen soup to the pot and cook for 5 minutes to release some liquid. Press "Cancel." Follow step 4, but cook for 12 to 17 minutes.

HEARTY ITALIAN SOUP

Sausage, potatoes, kale, and lots more veggies work together to make this Italian-style soup deeply flavorful, satisfying, and quite nutritious. Cutting the potatoes into small pieces is really important for the soup to cook at the right rate.

1 to 2 tablespoons avocado oil or olive oil

1 pound all-natural mild Italian sausage meat (pork, turkey, or chicken)

1 cup diced onion

1 cup diced carrots

1 cup diced celery

Pinch of red pepper flakes

Salt and ground black pepper

3 garlic cloves, minced

1 teaspoon Italian seasoning

1 (14.5-ounce) can fire-roasted or regular diced or crushed tomatoes, with their juices

4 cups low-sodium chicken broth, homemade (see page 240) or store-bought

3 cups ½-inch-diced peeled russet potatoes (2 to 3 small or medium potatoes)

1 bay leaf

4 to 6 cups chopped stemmed kale leaves

Grated or shredded Parmesan cheese, for serving* (optional)

*Omit if making the dairy-free option.

Slow Cooker • MAKES: 6 TO 8 SERVINGS

MAKE IT NOW

1   In a large skillet, heat 2 teaspoons of the oil over medium-high heat until shimmery. Add the sausage and cook, breaking it up as it cooks, until cooked through, about 5 minutes. Transfer to a paper towel–lined plate to drain.

2   Add the remaining oil to the skillet, if needed. Add the onion, carrots, and celery and cook, stirring, until soft, 4 to 5 minutes, seasoning with the red pepper flakes and lightly with salt and black pepper while they cook and stirring in the garlic and Italian seasoning during the last 30 to 60 seconds of cooking. *(Freezing instructions begin here.)*

3   Transfer the sausage and veggie mixture to the slow cooker and stir in the tomatoes, broth, potatoes, bay leaf, ½ teaspoon salt, and ¼ teaspoon black pepper.

4   Cover and cook on Low for 7 to 8 hours, until the potatoes are very tender.

5   Stir in the kale, cover, and cook on High until tender, 20 to 30 minutes.

6   Discard the bay leaf. Taste and season with salt and black pepper. Serve in bowls, topped with (optional) Parmesan.

(CONTINUES)

FREEZE FOR LATER: Follow steps 1 and 2. Let the sausage and veggie mixture cool, then transfer them to a gallon-size freezer bag or container and add the tomatoes, broth, potatoes, bay leaf, ½ teaspoon salt, and ¼ teaspoon black pepper. Seal and freeze.

PREPARE FROM FROZEN: *Note: You will need to have kale, salt, pepper, and (optional) Parmesan on hand to complete this meal.* Thaw. Transfer the soup to the slow cooker and follow steps 4 through 6.

Instant Pot • MAKES: 6 TO 8 SERVINGS

MAKE IT NOW

1   Set the 6-quart Instant Pot to "Sauté." Pour 2 teaspoons of the oil into the pot and heat until shimmery. Add the sausage and cook, breaking it up as it cooks, until cooked through, about 5 minutes. Transfer to a paper towel–lined plate to drain.

2   Pour the remaining oil into the Instant Pot, if needed, and heat until shimmery. Add the onion, carrots, and celery and cook, stirring, until soft, about 5 minutes, seasoning with the red pepper flakes and lightly with salt and black pepper while they cook and stirring in the garlic and Italian seasoning during the last 30 to 60 seconds of cooking. Press "Cancel."

3   Stir in the sausage, tomatoes, broth, potatoes, bay leaf, ½ teaspoon salt, and ¼ teaspoon pepper. *(Freezing instructions begin here.)*

4   Lock and seal the lid. Cook at high pressure for 7 minutes, then quick release the pressure.

5   Stir the kale into the soup. Set the Instant Pot to "Sauté" and cook until the kale is wilted, 3 to 5 minutes. Press "Cancel."

6   Discard the bay leaf. Taste and season with salt and pepper. Serve in bowls, topped with (optional) Parmesan.

FREEZE FOR LATER: Follow steps 1 through 3. Carefully transfer the uncooked soup to a gallon-size freezer bag or round container. Seal and freeze.

PREPARE FROM FROZEN: *Note: You will need to have kale, salt, pepper, and (optional) Parmesan on hand to complete this meal.* Set the Instant Pot to "Sauté." Transfer the frozen soup to the pot and cook for 5 minutes to release some liquid. Press "Cancel." Follow step 4, but cook the soup for 12 to 17 minutes. Follow steps 5 and 6.

TURKEY CHILI
WITH SWEET POTATO AND BLACK BEANS

Our lean turkey chili is not only hearty and absolutely delicious, but it's also chock-full of fiber, protein, and nutrients. The jalapeño lends just the right amount of heat without being overpowering. It's perfect for a comforting weeknight dinner, and you'll have leftovers for lunch the next day. Be sure to top it with your favorite chili toppings.

3 tablespoons avocado oil or olive oil

3 cups diced peeled sweet potatoes (about 3 medium)

Salt and ground black pepper

1 large onion, finely diced

4 garlic cloves, minced

1 teaspoon minced seeded jalapeño pepper

1 pound 99% lean ground turkey

2 cups low-sodium chicken broth, homemade (see page 240) or store-bought

1 (14- to 15-ounce) can petite diced tomatoes, with their juices

1 tablespoon tomato paste

1 (15-ounce) can black beans, drained and rinsed

1 tablespoon chili powder

1 tablespoon ground cumin

1 teaspoon paprika

¼ teaspoon dried oregano

Slow Cooker • **MAKES: 6 SERVINGS**

MAKE IT NOW

1   In a large skillet, heat 2 tablespoons of the oil over medium-high heat until shimmery. Add the sweet potatoes and cook, stirring, for about 4 minutes, until they start to soften, seasoning lightly with salt and pepper while they cook. Transfer the sweet potato to the slow cooker.

2   In the same skillet, heat the remaining 1 tablespoon oil over medium-high heat. Add the onion, garlic, jalapeño, and ground turkey and cook, stirring and breaking up the meat as it cooks, until the meat is cooked through and no longer pink and the onion has softened, about 5 minutes, seasoning lightly with salt and pepper as the mixture cooks. *(Freezing instructions begin here.)*

3   Transfer the turkey mixture to the slow cooker and add the broth, tomatoes, tomato paste, beans, chili powder, cumin, paprika, oregano, 1 teaspoon salt, and ¼ teaspoon pepper. Stir until well combined.

4   Cover and cook on Low for 6 to 8 hours or on High for 3 to 4 hours.

5   Taste and season with salt and pepper and serve warm.

FREEZE FOR LATER: Follow step 1, but set the sweet potato aside to cool instead of transferring it to the slow cooker. Follow step 2; let the meat mixture cool. Transfer the sweet potatoes and meat mixture to a gallon-size freezer bag or container and add the broth, tomatoes, tomato paste, black beans, chili powder, cumin, paprika, oregano, 1 teaspoon salt, and ¼ teaspoon pepper. Seal, toss gently to combine, and freeze.

PREPARE FROM FROZEN: *Note: Have salt and pepper on hand to complete this meal.* Thaw. Transfer the chili to the slow cooker. Follow steps 4 and 5.

Instant Pot • MAKES: 6 SERVINGS

MAKE IT NOW

1 Set the 6-quart Instant Pot to "Sauté." Pour in 2 tablespoons of the oil and heat until shimmery. Add the sweet potatoes and cook, stirring, for about 4 minutes, until they start to soften, seasoning lightly with salt and pepper while they cook. Transfer the sweet potatoes to a plate and set aside.

2 Pour the remaining 1 tablespoon oil into the pot and heat until shimmery. Add the onion, garlic, jalapeño, and ground turkey and cook, stirring and breaking up the meat as it cooks, until the meat is cooked through and no longer pink and the onion has softened, 5 to 7 minutes, seasoning lightly with salt and pepper as the mixture cooks. Press "Cancel."

3 Add the sweet potatoes, broth, tomatoes, tomato paste, beans, chili powder, cumin, paprika, oregano, 1 teaspoon salt, and ¼ teaspoon pepper to the pot and stir until well combined. *(Freezing instructions begin here.)*

4 Lock and seal the lid. Cook at high pressure for 7 minutes, then quick release the pressure.

5 Taste and season with salt and pepper and serve warm.

FREEZE FOR LATER: Follow steps 1 through 3. Carefully transfer the uncooked chili to a gallon-size freezer bag or round container. Seal and freeze (if using a freezer bag, set it in a bowl or round container with a diameter similar to the Instant Pot so it will fit in the pot when frozen; see page 22).

PREPARE FROM FROZEN: Set the Instant Pot to "Sauté." Transfer the frozen chili to the pot and cook for 5 minutes to release some liquid. Press "Cancel." Follow steps 4 and 5, but cook for 12 to 17 minutes.

AUTUMN CHOWDER

A reminder of the bountiful harvest at the beginning of fall, this chowder is filled to the brim with fresh produce. Another name for this soup could be "Comfort In a Bowl." The creamy richness, thanks to a bit of bacon, milk, and shredded cheddar, makes it great to serve to your loved ones on a crisp autumn or winter day.

Shortcuts: *Use your food processor's pulse setting to chop the onion, celery, and carrots into bite-size pieces.*

½ pound uncured bacon

2 cups diced onion (about 1 large)

2 cups diced celery (4 to 5 stalks)

2 cups diced carrots (about 6)

Salt and ground black pepper

2 garlic cloves, minced

3 cups low-sodium chicken broth, homemade (see page 240) or store-bought

4 cups ½-inch-diced peeled russet potatoes (about 4 medium)

1 cup frozen corn

1½ teaspoons minced fresh thyme leaves, or ½ teaspoon dried

2 bay leaves

4 tablespoons (½ stick) unsalted butter

¼ cup unbleached all-purpose flour

2 cups milk

Optional toppings: chopped fresh chives or parsley, oyster crackers, shredded cheddar cheese

---

Slow Cooker • MAKES: 6 TO 8 SERVINGS

MAKE IT NOW

1   In a large skillet, fry the bacon over medium-high heat until crisp on both sides. Transfer to a paper towel–lined plate, leaving the bacon grease in the pan. Chop the bacon into small pieces and set aside in the refrigerator.

2   Add the onion, celery, and carrots to the pan with the bacon grease and cook over medium-high heat, stirring and scraping up any browned bits from the bottom of the pan, until softened, 5 to 7 minutes, seasoning lightly with salt and pepper as they cook and stirring in the garlic during the last 30 to 60 seconds of cooking. *(Freezing instructions begin here.)*

3   Transfer the veggie mixture to the slow cooker and add the broth, potatoes, corn, thyme, bay leaves, 1 teaspoon salt, and ¼ teaspoon pepper.

(CONTINUES)

4   Cover and cook on Low for about 8 hours, or until the potatoes are very
    tender. Discard the bay leaves.

5   In a medium saucepan, melt the butter over medium-high heat. Add the flour
    and cook, whisking, for about 1 minute. Add the milk and cook, whisking
    almost continuously, until thickened, 3 to 4 minutes. Remove from the heat.

6   Stir the milk mixture and bacon bits into the chowder. Taste and season with
    salt and pepper. Serve with your favorite toppings.

FREEZE FOR LATER: Follow steps 1 and 2; let the bacon and veggie mixture cool.
Transfer the veggies to a gallon-size freezer bag or container and add the broth,
potatoes, corn, thyme, bay leaves, 1 teaspoon salt, and ¼ teaspoon pepper. Seal
and toss gently to combine, making sure the potatoes are completely submerged
in the liquid to avoid browning. Freeze. Place the bacon in a separate small
freezer bag or container. Seal and freeze alongside the soup.

PREPARE FROM FROZEN: *Note: You will need to have butter, flour, milk, salt,
pepper, and your favorite toppings on hand to complete this meal.* Thaw. Keep the
bacon in the refrigerator until needed. Transfer the chowder to the slow cooker
and follow steps 4 through 6.

Instant Pot • MAKES: 6 TO 8 SERVINGS

MAKE IT NOW

1   Place the bacon in the 6-quart Instant Pot and set the pot to "Sauté." Fry the
    bacon until crisp on both sides. Transfer the bacon to a paper towel–lined
    plate, leaving the bacon grease in the pot. Chop the bacon into small pieces
    and set aside in the refrigerator.

2   Add the onion, carrots, and celery to the pot and cook over medium-high
    heat, stirring and scraping up any browned bits from the bottom of the pot,
    until softened, 8 to 10 minutes, seasoning lightly with salt and pepper as they
    cook and stirring in the garlic during the last 30 to 60 seconds of cooking.
    Press "Cancel."

3   Stir in the broth, potatoes, corn, thyme, bay leaves, 1 teaspoon salt, and
    ¼ teaspoon pepper. *(Freezing instructions begin here.)*

4   Lock and seal the lid. Cook at high pressure for 7 minutes, then quick release
    the pressure. Discard the bay leaves.

5   In a medium saucepan, melt the butter over medium-high heat. Add the flour and cook, whisking, for about 1 minute. Add the milk and cook, whisking almost continuously, until thickened, 3 to 4 minutes. Remove from the heat.

6   Stir the milk mixture and bacon bits into the chowder. Taste and season with salt and pepper. Serve with your favorite toppings.

FREEZE FOR LATER: Follow steps 1 through 3. Carefully transfer the uncooked soup to a gallon-size freezer bag or container. Seal, making sure the potatoes are completely submerged in the liquid to prevent browning, and freeze (if using a freezer bag, set it in a bowl or round container with a diameter similar to the Instant Pot so it will fit in the pot when frozen; see page 22). Place the bacon in a separate small freezer bag or container. Seal and freeze alongside the soup.

PREPARE FROM FROZEN: *Note: You will need to have butter, flour, milk, salt, pepper, and your favorite toppings on hand to complete this meal.* Thaw the bacon. Set the Instant Pot to "Sauté." Transfer the frozen soup to the pot and cook for 5 minutes to release some liquid. Press "Cancel." Follow step 4, but cook for 12 to 17 minutes. Follow steps 5 and 6.

POTLUCK PUMPKIN CHILI

Pumpkin chili is perfect for a fall potluck or tailgate party. This one is filled with a variety of vegetables, beans, and warm spices, satisfying both meat-eaters and vegetarians alike. You can also fully cook this big batch, divide it into small freezer containers, and enjoy it as a nutritious lunch at work or home.

1 to 2 tablespoons avocado oil or olive oil

1 onion, diced (about 1 cup)

2 carrots, diced (about 1 cup)

4 garlic cloves, minced

Pinch of red pepper flakes

4 cups low-sodium vegetable broth or chicken broth, homemade (see page 240) or store-bought

1 (28-ounce) can diced tomatoes, with their juices

1 (15-ounce) can pumpkin puree

2 tablespoons tomato paste

1 (15-ounce) can black beans, drained and rinsed

1 (15-ounce) can pinto beans, drained and rinsed

1 (15-ounce) can chickpeas, drained and rinsed

2 tablespoons chili powder

1 tablespoon ground cumin

½ teaspoon dried oregano

½ teaspoon paprika

1 teaspoon salt, plus more to taste

½ teaspoon ground black pepper, plus more to taste

Optional toppings: diced avocado, sour cream or plain Greek yogurt,* shredded cheddar cheese,* crushed corn tortilla chips, thinly sliced green onions

Omit if making a dairy-free version.

Slow Cooker • MAKES: 8 TO 10 SERVINGS

MAKE IT NOW

1   In a large skillet, heat the oil over medium-high heat until shimmery. Add the onion and carrots and cook, stirring, until tender, 4 to 5 minutes, stirring in the garlic and red pepper flakes during the last 30 to 60 seconds of cooking. *(Freezing instructions begin here.)*

2   Transfer the veggie mixture to the slow cooker and add the broth, tomatoes, pumpkin, tomato paste, black beans, pinto beans, chickpeas, chili powder, cumin, oregano, paprika, 1 teaspoon salt, and ½ teaspoon pepper. Stir to combine. Cover and cook on Low for 6 to 8 hours or on High for 3 to 4 hours.

3   Taste and season with more salt and black pepper. Serve warm, with your favorite toppings.

FREEZE FOR LATER: Follow step 1. Let the veggie mixture cool, then transfer it to one or two gallon-size freezer bags or containers and add the remaining ingredients (except the optional toppings). Seal and freeze.

PREPARE FROM FROZEN: *Note: Have salt, pepper, and your favorite toppings on hand to complete this meal.* Thaw. Transfer the chili to the slow cooker and follow steps 2 and 3.

Instant Pot • MAKES: 8 TO 10 SERVINGS

MAKE IT NOW

1   Set the 6-quart Instant Pot to "Sauté." Pour the oil into the pot and heat until shimmery. Add the onion and carrots and cook, stirring, until tender, 4 to 5 minutes, stirring in the garlic and red pepper flakes during the last 30 to 60 seconds of cooking. Press "Cancel." Add the broth, tomatoes, pumpkin, tomato paste, black beans, pinto beans, chickpeas, chili powder, cumin, oregano, paprika, 1 teaspoon salt, and ½ teaspoon pepper and stir to combine. *(Freezing instructions begin here.)*

2   Lock and seal the lid. Cook at high pressure for 7 minutes, then quick release the pressure.

3   Taste and season with more salt and black pepper. Serve warm, with your favorite toppings.

FREEZE FOR LATER: Follow step 1. Carefully transfer the uncooked chili to one or two gallon-size freezer bags or round containers. Seal and freeze (if using freezer bags, set each one in a bowl or round container with a diameter similar to the Instant Pot so they will fit in the pot when frozen; see page 22).

PREPARE FROM FROZEN: *Note: Have salt, pepper, and your favorite toppings on hand to complete this meal.* Set the Instant Pot to "Sauté." Transfer the frozen chili to the pot and cook for 5 to 10 minutes to release some liquid. Press "Cancel." Follow step 2, but cook for 12 to 17 minutes. Follow step 3.

VEGETARIAN TORTILLA SOUP

Before you is one of the easiest recipes in our book. This broth-based vegetarian soup may be lighter fare, but your appetite will be more than satisfied thanks to the hearty beans, brown rice, veggies, and bold flavors. Our recipe team gave it rave reviews! We did notice in our tests that this soup thickens up a lot over time, as the rice soaks up the liquid. You can always add more broth to thin it out the next day. If you have a heat-sensitive palate, cut back on the taco seasoning by 1 tablespoon and use a mild salsa.

Shortcut: *Freeze leftover cooked brown rice to have on hand to use in this soup.*

4 cups vegetable broth or chicken broth, homemade (see page 240) or store-bought

1 (15-ounce) can vegetarian refried beans

1 (15-ounce) can black beans, drained and rinsed

1 (15-ounce) can corn, drained

1 (15-ounce) can petite diced tomatoes, with their juices

1 (4-ounce) can diced green chiles, with their juices

1 cup mild or medium salsa

2 tablespoons taco seasoning, homemade (see page 243) or store-bought

1 to 2 cups cooked brown rice

Optional toppings: lime wedges, diced avocado, shredded cheddar cheese,* minced jalapeños, sour cream or plain Greek yogurt,* crushed tortilla chips

Omit if making a dairy-free version.

Slow Cooker • MAKES: 6 TO 8 SERVINGS

MAKE IT NOW

1   *(Freezing instructions begin here.)* In the slow cooker, combine the broth, refried beans, black beans, corn, tomatoes, chiles, salsa, and taco seasoning and stir to combine, breaking up the refried beans as much as possible.

2   Cover and cook on Low for 6 to 8 hours.

3   Stir the cooked rice into the soup. Serve warm, with your favorite toppings. (The soup will thicken as it sits.)

FREEZE FOR LATER: In a large bowl, stir together all the ingredients except the rice and optional toppings, breaking up the refried beans as much as possible. Carefully ladle the uncooked soup into one or two gallon-size freezer bags or containers. Seal and freeze. Place the cooked rice in a separate small freezer bag or container. Seal and freeze alongside the soup.

(CONTINUES)

PREPARE FROM FROZEN: *Note: Have your favorite toppings on hand to complete this meal.* Thaw. Transfer the soup to the slow cooker and follow steps 2 and 3.

Instant Pot • MAKES: 6 TO 8 SERVINGS

MAKE IT NOW

1 In the 6-quart Instant Pot, combine the broth, refried beans, black beans, corn, tomatoes, chiles, salsa, and taco seasoning and stir to combine, breaking up the refried beans as much as possible. *(Freezing instructions begin here.)*

2 Lock and seal the lid. Cook at high pressure for 7 minutes, then quick release the pressure.

3 Stir in the cooked rice. Serve warm, with your favorite toppings. (The soup will thicken as it sits.)

FREEZE FOR LATER: Follow step 1. Carefully ladle the soup into one or two gallon-size freezer bags or round containers. Seal and freeze (if using a freezer bag, set it in a bowl or round container with a diameter similar to the Instant Pot so it will fit in the pot when frozen; see page 22). Place the cooked rice in a separate small freezer bag or container. Seal and freeze alongside the soup.

PREPARE FROM FROZEN: *Note: Have your favorite toppings on hand to complete this meal.* At least partially thaw the rice. Set the Instant Pot to "Sauté." Transfer the frozen soup to the pot and cook for 5 minutes to release some liquid. Press "Cancel." Follow steps 2 and 3, but cook for 12 to 17 minutes.

WHITE CHICKEN CHILI

Thanks to bell and jalapeño peppers, fresh lime juice, and a blend of warm spices, this lighter chili comes out of the cooker bright, creamy, and a little spicy. Pair with corn bread and serve with garnishes like lime wedges, diced avocado, and crushed tortilla chips. Don't skip the sauté step at the beginning, though; browning the aromatics and blooming the spices builds big flavor.

Shortcut: *Use a 7-ounce can mild diced green chiles in place of the jalapeños.*

2 (14.5-ounce) cans cannellini or great northern beans, drained and rinsed

1 to 2 tablespoons avocado oil or olive oil

1 onion, diced (about 1 cup)

2 medium jalapeño peppers, minced

2 medium green bell peppers, diced

Salt and ground black pepper

4 garlic cloves, minced

1 tablespoon ground cumin

1½ teaspoons ground coriander

1 teaspoon chili powder

4 cups (for slow cooker) or 3 cups (for Instant Pot) low-sodium chicken broth, homemade (see page 240) or store-bought

Juice of 2 limes

1½ pounds boneless, skinless medium chicken breasts

2 tablespoons finely chopped fresh cilantro or parsley

Lime wedges, for serving

Optional toppings: diced avocado, crushed tortilla chips, sour cream,* shredded Monterey Jack cheese*

Omit if making a dairy-free version.

Slow Cooker • MAKES: 6 SERVINGS

MAKE IT NOW

1   In a medium bowl, mash half the beans with a potato masher or fork until chunky and set aside.

2   In a large skillet, heat the oil over medium-high heat until shimmery. Add onion, jalapeños, and bell peppers and cook, stirring, until softened, 5 to 7 minutes, seasoning with salt and black pepper while they cook and stirring in the garlic, cumin, coriander, and chili powder during the last 30 to 60 seconds of cooking. *(Freezing instructions begin here.)*

3   Transfer the veggie mixture to the slow cooker and add the broth, lime juice, chicken breasts, all the beans, 1 teaspoon salt, and ¼ teaspoon black pepper. Stir to combine.

(CONTINUES)

4   Cover and cook on Low for 3 to 4 hours, until the chicken is cooked through. (The chicken is done when it is no longer pink inside and/or registers 165°F internally.) Transfer the chicken to a cutting board and shred with two forks or chop into bite-size pieces. Return the chicken to the cooker and stir in the cilantro or parsley.

5   Taste and season with salt and black pepper. Serve warm, with lime wedges on the side and your favorite toppings.

FREEZE FOR LATER: Follow steps 1 and 2. Let the veggie mixture cool, then transfer all the beans and veggie mixture to a gallon-size freezer bag or container and add the broth, lime juice, chicken breasts, 1 teaspoon salt, and ¼ teaspoon black pepper. Seal and freeze.

PREPARE FROM FROZEN: *Note: You will need to have cilantro or parsley, salt, pepper, lime wedges, and your favorite toppings on hand to complete this meal.* Thaw. Transfer the chili to the slow cooker and follow steps 4 and 5.

Instant Pot • MAKES: 6 SERVINGS

MAKE IT NOW

1   In a medium bowl, mash half the beans with a potato masher or fork until chunky and set aside.

2   Set the 6-quart Instant Pot to "Sauté." Pour the oil into the pot and heat until shimmery. Add onion, jalapeños, and bell peppers and cook, stirring, until softened, about 5 minutes, seasoning with salt and black pepper while they cook and stirring in the garlic, cumin, coriander, and chili powder during the last 30 to 60 seconds of cooking. Press "Cancel."

3   Stir in the broth, lime juice, chicken breasts, all the beans, 1 teaspoon salt, and ¼ teaspoon black pepper. *(Freezing instructions begin here.)*

4   Lock and seal the lid. Cook at high pressure for 6 minutes, then quick release the pressure. Transfer the chicken to a cutting board and shred with two forks or chop into bite-size pieces. Return the chicken to the pot and stir in the cilantro or parsley.

5   Taste and season with salt and black pepper. Serve warm, with lime wedges on the side and your favorite toppings.

FREEZE FOR LATER: Follow steps 1 through 3. Carefully transfer the uncooked soup to one or two gallon-size freezer bags or round containers (do not stack the chicken in the bag/container; instead, place them side by side). Seal and freeze (if using freezer bags, set each one in a bowl or round container with a diameter similar to the Instant Pot so they will fit in the pot when frozen; see page 22).

PREPARE FROM FROZEN: *Note: You will need to have cilantro or parsley, salt, pepper, lime wedges, and your favorite toppings on hand to complete this meal.* Set the Instant Pot to "Sauté." Transfer the frozen chili to the pot and cook for 5 minutes to release some liquid. Press "Cancel." Follow step 4, but cook for 17 to 22 minutes. Follow step 5.

BARLEY AND CHICKPEA SOUP

Contributed by Liz Weiss of Liz's Healthy Table

This hearty barley and chickpea soup has a lovely flavor, meaty texture, and an I-need-to-slurp-this-soup-NOW aroma! At the market, look for pearl barley—it cooks up faster, because the tough bran layer is partially removed—and feel free to swap out the chickpeas for any other favorite bean. Vegans can omit the Parmesan cheese used for topping.

1 tablespoon avocado oil or olive oil

1 (8-ounce) package sliced mushrooms, coarsely chopped

1 small onion, diced

Kosher salt and ground black pepper

4 cups low-sodium vegetable broth

1 (14.5-ounce) can fire-roasted petite diced tomatoes

1 (15-ounce) can chickpeas, drained and rinsed

3 carrots, sliced lengthwise and cut into ¼-inch-thick pieces (about 1½ cups)

⅓ cup pearl barley

6 sprigs fresh thyme

Optional toppings: grated Parmesan cheese,* chopped fresh parsley

Omit if making a dairy-free version.

Slow Cooker • **MAKES: 6 SERVINGS**

MAKE IT NOW

1   In a large nonstick skillet, heat the oil over medium-high heat until shimmery. Add the mushrooms and onion and cook, stirring frequently, until softened, about 7 minutes. Season with salt and pepper.

2   Transfer the mushroom mixture to the slow cooker and add the broth, tomatoes, chickpeas, carrots, barley, and thyme. Stir to combine.

3   Cover and cook on Low for 6 to 8 hours, until the carrots are tender. Discard the thyme sprigs. Taste and season with salt and pepper. (*Freezing instructions begin here.*)

4   Serve warm, in individual bowls, topped with Parmesan and parsley, if desired.

FREEZE FOR LATER: Follow steps 1 through 3. Let the soup cool completely, then transfer to a gallon-size freezer bag or container. Seal and freeze.

PREPARE FROM FROZEN: *Note: You may want to have (optional) Parmesan and parsley on hand to complete this meal.* Thaw. Transfer the soup to the slow cooker and reheat on Low, stirring occasionally; alternatively, reheat the soup in a saucepan over medium-low heat, stirring occasionally, or in the microwave. Follow step 4.

Instant Pot • MAKES: 6 SERVINGS

MAKE IT NOW

1   Set the 6-quart Instant Pot to "Sauté." Pour the oil into the pot and heat until shimmery. Add the mushrooms and onion and cook, stirring frequently, until the vegetables have softened, about 7 minutes. Season with salt and pepper. Press "Cancel."

2   Add the broth, tomatoes, chickpeas, carrots, barley, and thyme and stir to combine. Lock and seal the lid. Cook at high pressure for 7 minutes, then quick release the pressure. Discard the thyme sprigs. Taste and season with salt and pepper. *(Freezing instructions begin here.)*

3   Serve warm, in individual bowls, topped with Parmesan and parsley, if desired.

FREEZE FOR LATER: Follow steps 1 and 2. Let the soup cool completely, then transfer to a gallon-size freezer bag or container. Seal and freeze (if using a freezer bag, set it in a bowl or round container with a diameter similar to the Instant Pot so it will fit in the pot when frozen; see page 22).

PREPARE FROM FROZEN: *Note: You may want to have (optional) Parmesan and parsley on hand to complete this meal.* Set the Instant Pot to "Sauté." Transfer the frozen soup to the pot and cook for 5 minutes to release some liquid. Press "Cancel." Lock and seal the lid. Cook at high pressure for 5 minutes, then quick release the pressure. If the soup is not fully warmed through, cook for 1 to 2 minutes more. Follow step 3.

Fake-Out Lasagna,
page 214

pastas, salads & more

WEEKNIGHT MEATY MARINARA SAUCE

This satisfying meat sauce is incredibly versatile. The sausage is the heavy-hitter ingredient that really ramps up the flavor. Serve over your favorite pasta, zoodles, or even steamed veggies, with a little Parmesan cheese on top. This recipe can also be fully cooked and frozen in small portions. So many options!

1 to 2 tablespoons avocado oil or olive oil

1 yellow onion, finely diced (about 1 cup)

2 garlic cloves, minced

½ pound lean ground beef

½ pound mild ground Italian sausage or Italian turkey sausage

⅛ teaspoon red pepper flakes

Salt and ground black pepper

2 (24-ounce) jars marinara sauce, or 6 cups Marvelous Marinara Sauce (page 216)

Cooked whole-grain pasta,* zoodles, or steamed veggies, for serving

Grated Parmesan cheese,** for serving (optional)

*Omit if making a gluten-free version.

**Omit if making a dairy-free version.

Slow Cooker • MAKES: 6 SERVINGS

MAKE IT NOW

1   In a large skillet, heat the oil over medium-high heat until shimmery. Add the onion and cook, stirring, until soft, 4 to 5 minutes, stirring in the garlic the last 30 to 60 seconds of cooking. Add the ground beef and sausage and cook, breaking up the meat as it cooks, until browned, 5 to 7 minutes, seasoning lightly with the red pepper flakes, salt, and black pepper while it cooks. Drain the grease from the pan. *(Freezing instructions begin here.)*

2   Transfer the meat mixture to the slow cooker and stir in the marinara sauce.

3   Cover and cook on Low for 6 to 8 hours. If the edges start to burn a little, just give it a stir.

4   Serve the sauce over whole-grain pasta, zoodles, or steamed veggies, topped with Parmesan, if desired.

(CONTINUES)

FREEZE FOR LATER: Follow step 1. Let the meat mixture cool, then transfer it to a gallon-size freezer bag or container and pour in the marinara. Seal, gently toss to combine, and freeze.

PREPARE FROM FROZEN: *Note: You will need to have cooked whole-grain pasta, zoodles, or steamed veggies and (optional) Parmesan on hand to complete this meal.* Thaw. Transfer the sauce to the slow cooker and follow steps 3 and 4.

Instant Pot • MAKES: 6 SERVINGS

MAKE IT NOW

1   Set the 6-quart Instant Pot to "Sauté." Pour the oil into the pot and heat until shimmery. Add the onion and cook, stirring, for 4 to 5 minutes, until softened, stirring in the garlic during the last 30 to 60 seconds of cooking. Add the ground beef and sausage and cook, breaking up the meat as it cooks, until browned, 5 to 7 minutes, seasoning lightly with the red pepper flakes, salt, and black pepper while it cooks. Using pot holders, carefully lift the inner pot and drain off the grease.

2   Add the marinara sauce to the meat mixture and stir to combine. Press "Cancel." *(Freezing instructions begin here.)*

3   Lock and seal the lid. Cook at high pressure for 5 minutes, then quick release the pressure.

4   Serve the sauce over whole-grain pasta, zoodles, or steamed veggies, topped with Parmesan, if desired.

FREEZE FOR LATER: Follow steps 1 and 2. Pour the meat sauce into a gallon-size freezer bag or round container. Seal and freeze (if using a freezer bag, set it in a bowl or round container with a diameter similar to the Instant Pot so it will fit in the pot when frozen; see page 20).

PREPARE FROM FROZEN: *Note: You will need to have cooked whole-grain pasta, zoodles, or steamed veggies and (optional) Parmesan on hand to complete this meal.* Set the Instant Pot to "Sauté." Transfer the frozen sauce to the pot and cook for 5 minutes to release some liquid. Press "Cancel." Follow step 3, but cook for 10 to 15 minutes. Follow step 4.

CHICKEN PARMESAN PASTA

There are three good reasons why this pasta dish was the first recipe I developed for my Instant Pot years ago and why I still make it today—it's easy, tasty, and healthy. Our recipe testing team also deemed it one of the most popular ones with their kids. With only five main ingredients, not only does it make a busy weeknight meal a cinch, but it really stretches a buck, too. To up the nutritional ante even more, stir in baby spinach, steamed broccoli, or any other cooked veggies you love at the end before adding the cheese. —Rachel

3½ cups Marvelous Marinara Sauce (page 216) or store-bought

1 to 1¼ pounds boneless, skinless medium chicken breasts

8 ounces whole-wheat rotini pasta

Olive oil (for slow cooker)

½ cup shredded or grated Parmesan cheese

1 cup shredded mozzarella cheese

Finely chopped fresh parsley or basil, for garnish (optional)

Slow Cooker • **MAKES: 4 SERVINGS**

MAKE IT NOW

1   *(Freezing instructions begin here.)* Pour the marinara sauce into the slow cooker. Submerge the chicken in the sauce.

2   Cover and cook on Low for 2½ to 3½ hours, until the chicken is cooked through. (The chicken is done when it is no longer pink inside and/or registers 165°F internally.)

3   About 20 minutes before the slow cooker is done, cook the pasta according to the package directions. Drain the pasta and return it to the pot. Toss with a little olive oil to prevent sticking, cover, and set aside.

4   Transfer the chicken to a cutting board and dice it or shred with two forks. Gently stir the chicken and cooked pasta into the sauce in the slow cooker. Sprinkle the Parmesan and mozzarella over the top and stir again.

5   Garnish with chopped fresh herbs, if desired. Serve warm.

(CONTINUES)

FREEZE FOR LATER: Place the marinara and chicken in a gallon-size freezer bag or container. Seal and freeze. Place the Parmesan and mozzarella cheeses in a separate smaller freezer bag or container. Seal and freeze alongside the chicken.

PREPARE FROM FROZEN: *Note: You will need to have whole-wheat rotini, olive oil, and (optional) parsley or basil on hand to complete this meal.* Thaw. Transfer the chicken and sauce to the slow cooker. Follow steps 2 through 5.

Instant Pot • MAKES: 4 SERVINGS

MAKE IT NOW

1   *(Freezing instructions begin here.)* Place the marinara sauce, chicken, pasta, and 1 cup water in the 6-quart Instant Pot. Stir, making sure the chicken and pasta are submerged in the sauce.

2   Lock and seal the lid. Cook at high pressure for 7 minutes, then quick release the pressure. Cover the spout with a dish towel to prevent splatters when releasing. (The chicken is done when it registers 165°F internally and is no longer pink inside.)

3   Transfer the chicken to a cutting board and dice it or shred with two forks. Return the chicken to the pot and gently stir to combine with the pasta and sauce. Sprinkle the Parmesan and mozzarella over the top and stir again.

4   Garnish with chopped fresh herbs, if desired. Serve warm.

FREEZE FOR LATER: Place the sauce and chicken in a gallon-size freezer bag or round container (do not stack the chicken breasts in the bag/container; instead, place them side by side). Seal and freeze (if using a freezer bag, set it in a bowl or round container with a diameter similar to the Instant Pot so it will fit in the pot when frozen; see page 22). Place the Parmesan and mozzarella cheeses in a separate smaller freezer bag or container. Seal and freeze alongside the chicken.

PREPARE FROM FROZEN: *Note: You will need to have whole-wheat rotini, olive oil, and (optional) parsley or basil on hand to complete this meal.* Thaw the cheeses. Set the Instant Pot to "Sauté." Transfer the frozen meal to the pot and cook for 5 minutes to release some liquid. Press "Cancel." Follow step 2, but cook for 15 to 20 minutes. While the chicken cooks, cook the pasta according to the package directions. Drain the pasta and return it to the pot. Toss with a little olive oil to prevent sticking, cover, and set aside. Follow steps 3 and 4.

FAKE-OUT LASAGNA

Mmmm . . . lasagna. We all love it. But sometimes we just don't have the time to make that multistep, layered deliciousness. Meet Fake-Out Lasagna. You still get the homemade meaty marinara sauce, but we took a shortcut by using ravioli for the pasta and cheese layers. For some added nutrition, you can toss a handful or two of baby spinach into the sauce before cooking it. Enjoy!

1 tablespoon avocado oil or olive oil

½ yellow or white onion, diced (about ½ cup)

2 garlic cloves, minced

½ pound lean ground beef

½ pound ground pork sausage meat

2 (24-ounce) jars marinara sauce, or 6 cups Marvelous Marinara Sauce (page 216)

20 ounces frozen cheese ravioli (look for an all-natural brand or one with recognizable ingredients)

2 cups shredded mozzarella cheese

Slow Cooker • MAKES: 4 TO 6 SERVINGS

MAKE IT NOW

1   In a large skillet, heat the oil over medium-high heat. Add the onion and cook, stirring, until softened, 3 to 4 minutes, stirring in the garlic during the last 30 to 60 seconds of cooking. Add the ground beef and sausage and cook, breaking up the meat as it cooks, until browned and no longer pink, 5 to 7 minutes. Drain the grease from the pan. *(Freezing instructions begin here.)*

2   Transfer the meat mixture to the slow cooker and pour in the marinara sauce. Stir to combine.

3   Cover and cook on Low for 3 to 5 hours. If the edges start to burn a little, just give it a stir.

4   Set the slow cooker to High. Add the ravioli and quickly stir to coat with the sauce. Sprinkle the cheese over the top. Cover and cook for 30 to 45 minutes, until the ravioli are warmed through (check one ravioli to make sure it's warm in the middle) and the cheese on top has melted. Serve warm.

FREEZE FOR LATER: Follow step 1. Let the meat mixture cool, then transfer it to a gallon-size freezer bag or container and pour in the marinara. Seal and freeze. Place the mozzarella in a small freezer bag or container. Seal and freeze alongside the meat sauce and the bag of frozen ravioli.

PREPARE FROM FROZEN: Thaw the meat sauce and cheese (do not thaw the ravioli). Place in the slow cooker. Follow steps 3 and 4.

Instant Pot • MAKES: 4 TO 6 SERVINGS

MAKE IT NOW

1   Set the 6-quart Instant Pot to "Sauté." Pour the oil into the pot and heat until shimmery. Add the onion and cook, stirring, until softened, 3 to 4 minutes, stirring in the garlic during the last 30 to 60 seconds of cooking. Add the ground beef and sausage and cook, breaking up the meat as it cooks, 5 to 7 minutes, until browned and no longer pink. Press "Cancel." Using pot holders, carefully lift the inner pot and drain off the grease. Add the marinara sauce to the meat mixture and stir to combine. *(Freezing instructions begin here.)*

2   Add the ravioli and stir to coat with the sauce. Lock and seal the lid. Cook at high pressure for 5 minutes, then quick release the pressure.

3   Sprinkle the mozzarella over the top. Place the lid back on the pot and let the meal sit on warm for 10 minutes to melt the cheese. Serve warm.

FREEZE FOR LATER: Follow step 1. Let the meat mixture cool, then transfer it to a gallon-size freezer bag or round container. Seal and freeze (if using a freezer bag, set it in a bowl or round container with a diameter similar to the Instant Pot so it will fit in the pot when frozen; see page 22). Place the mozzarella in a small freezer bag or container. Seal and freeze alongside the meat sauce and the bag of frozen ravioli.

PREPARE FROM FROZEN: Thaw the cheese (do not thaw the ravioli). Set the Instant Pot to "Sauté." Transfer the frozen sauce to the pot and cook for 5 minutes to release some liquid. Press "Cancel." Lock and seal the lid. Cook at high pressure for 10 to 15 minutes, then quick release the pressure. Follow steps 2 and 3.

MARVELOUS MARINARA SAUCE

Once you realize how easy it is to make homemade marinara sauce, you may never go back to the store-bought stuff again. You can adjust the seasoning according to your taste because you are in total control of the ingredients. Whether you make it in your slow cooker or Instant Pot, it will have that slow-cooked-all-day taste and your home will smell amazing. One batch makes a lot, so stock your freezer with mason jars or freezer bags of sauce to pull out and use in several of the recipes in this book.

1 tablespoon avocado oil or olive oil

1 yellow onion, diced (about 1 cup)

Salt and ground black pepper

2 garlic cloves, minced

Pinch of red pepper flakes

2 tablespoons tomato paste

2 (28-ounce) cans crushed tomatoes

1 teaspoon sugar

½ teaspoon dried oregano

2 tablespoons finely chopped fresh basil, or 2 teaspoons dried

2 tablespoons finely chopped fresh parsley, or 2 teaspoons dried

Cooked whole-grain pasta* or zoodles, for serving

Freshly grated Parmesan cheese,** for serving (optional)

*Omit if making a gluten-free version.

**Omit if making a dairy-free version.

Slow Cooker • MAKES: ABOUT 6 CUPS (10 TO 12 SERVINGS)

MAKE IT NOW

1   In a large skillet, heat the oil over medium-high heat until shimmery. Add the onion and cook, stirring, until softened, 4 to 5 minutes, seasoning with salt and black pepper while they cook. Stir in the garlic, red pepper flakes, and tomato paste and cook for 30 to 60 seconds more, until fragrant. *(Freezing instructions begin here.)*

2   Transfer the onion mixture to the slow cooker and add the crushed tomatoes, sugar, oregano, basil, parsley, and 1½ teaspoons salt.

3   Cover and cook on Low for 9 to 11 hours or on High for 5 to 7 hours.

4   Taste and season with salt and black pepper. Serve over your favorite whole-grain pasta or zoodles, topped with freshly grated Parmesan, if desired.

(CONTINUES)

FREEZE FOR LATER: Follow step 1. Let the onion mixture cool, then transfer to a gallon-size freezer bag or container and add the crushed tomatoes, sugar, oregano, basil, parsley, and 1½ teaspoons salt. Seal, toss gently to combine, and freeze.

PREPARE FROM FROZEN: *Note: You will need to have salt, pepper, cooked whole-grain pasta or zoodles, and (optional) Parmesan on hand to complete this meal.* Thaw. Transfer the sauce to the slow cooker and follow steps 3 and 4.

Instant Pot • MAKES: ABOUT 6 CUPS (10 TO 12 SERVINGS)

MAKE IT NOW

1   Set the 6-quart Instant Pot to "Sauté." Pour the oil into the pot and heat until shimmery. Add the onion and cook, stirring, until softened, 4 to 5 minutes, seasoning with salt and black pepper while they cook. Stir in the garlic, red pepper flakes, and tomato paste and cook for 30 to 60 seconds more, until fragrant. Press "Cancel."

2   Stir in the crushed tomatoes, sugar, oregano, basil, parsley, and 1½ teaspoons salt. *(Freezing instructions begin here.)*

3   Lock and seal the lid. Cook at high pressure for 10 minutes, then quick release the pressure.

4   Taste and season with salt and black pepper. Serve over your favorite whole-grain pasta or zoodles, topped with freshly grated Parmesan, if desired.

FREEZE FOR LATER: *Note: You will need to have salt, pepper, cooked whole-grain pasta or zoodles, and (optional) Parmesan on hand to complete this meal.* Follow steps 1 and 2. Carefully transfer the uncooked sauce to a gallon-size freezer bag or container. Seal and freeze (if using a freezer bag, set it in a bowl or round container with a diameter similar to the Instant Pot so it will fit in the pot when frozen; see page 22).

PREPARE FROM FROZEN: Set the Instant Pot to "Sauté." Transfer the frozen sauce to the pot and cook for 5 minutes to release some liquid. Press "Cancel." Follow step 3, but cook for 10 to 15 minutes. Follow step 4.

VEGGIE-AND-BEAN-STUFFED BURRITOS

These budget-friendly burritos boast so many veggies, including onions, peppers, mushrooms, and tomatoes. In combination with the heart-healthy beans, these make for a super-satisfying lunch or dinner. They do have a kick to them, but you can always leave out the taco seasoning or pull back on the salsa. Feel free to add some cooked brown rice to the filling to make these stretch even further.

1 small onion, finely diced (about 1 cup)

1 green bell pepper, diced (about 1 cup)

1 cup diced fresh mushrooms

1 cup frozen corn or drained canned corn

1 (15-ounce ounce) can black beans, drained and rinsed

1 (15-ounce ounce) can pinto beans or kidney beans, drained and rinsed

1 (14.5-ounce ounce) can fire-roasted diced tomatoes, drained

1 cup mild salsa (or use medium to add more heat)

1 tablespoon taco seasoning, homemade (see page 243) or store-bought

6 to 8 burrito-size whole-wheat tortillas*

1½ to 2 cups shredded cheddar cheese, or more to taste

Optional toppings: sour cream, guacamole, salsa, lettuce, etc.

Use gluten-free wraps or corn tortillas for a gluten-free version.

Slow Cooker • MAKES: 6 TO 8 LARGE BURRITOS

MAKE IT NOW

1   *(Freezing instructions begin here.)* Place the onion, bell pepper, mushrooms, corn, black beans, pinto beans, tomatoes, salsa, and taco seasoning in the slow cooker and stir to combine.

2   Cover and cook on Low for 6 to 8 hours, until the onion is softened.

3   Arrange the tortillas on a flat surface. Use a slotted spoon to top each tortilla with 1 cup of the veggie-bean mixture. Top each with ¼ cup of the cheese (or more, to your preference). Roll up the tortillas like a burrito and serve with your favorite toppings.

(CONTINUES)

FREEZE FOR LATER: Combine the onion, bell pepper, mushrooms, corn, black beans, pinto beans, tomatoes, salsa, and taco seasoning in a gallon-size freezer bag or container. Seal, toss a little to combine, and freeze. Place the tortillas and cheese in separate freezer bags or containers. Seal and freeze alongside the veggie mixture.

PREPARE FROM FROZEN: *Note: Have your favorite toppings on hand to complete this meal.* Thaw. Place the veggie mixture in the slow cooker and follow steps 2 and 3.

Instant Pot • MAKES: 6 TO 8 LARGE BURRITOS

MAKE IT NOW

1   *(Freezing instructions begin here.)* Place the onion, bell pepper, mushrooms, corn, black beans, pinto beans, tomatoes, salsa, and taco seasoning in the 6-quart Instant Pot and stir to combine.

2   Lock and seal the lid. Cook at high pressure for 12 minutes, then quick release the pressure.

3   Arrange the tortillas on a flat surface. Use a slotted spoon to top each tortilla with 1 cup of the veggie-bean mixture. Top each with ¼ cup of the cheese (or more, to your preference). Roll up the tortillas like a burrito and serve with your favorite toppings.

FREEZE FOR LATER: Combine the onion, bell pepper, mushrooms, corn, black beans, pinto beans, tomatoes, salsa, and taco seasoning in a gallon-size freezer bag or container. Seal, toss a little to combine, and freeze. Place the tortillas and cheese in separate freezer bags or containers. Seal and freeze alongside the veggie mixture.

PREPARE FROM FROZEN: *Note: Have your favorite toppings on hand to complete this meal.* Thaw the tortillas and cheese. Set the Instant Pot to "Sauté." Transfer the frozen veggie mixture to the pot and cook for 5 minutes to release some liquid. Press "Cancel." Follow step 2, but cook for 10 to 15 minutes. Follow step 3.

CHICKEN COBB SALAD

Cobb Salad is always a win, in our opinion. This savory dressing is a longtime favorite, especially once it mingles with the ripe avocado and Gorgonzola cheese in the salad. Since children may not be big fans of salad yet, you can serve the components separately at dinner so everyone is happy. To make the prep even easier, you can find recipes on our website (thrivinghome.org) for "Easy-to-Peel Hard-Boiled Eggs in the Instant Pot" and "The No-Fail Way to Cook Bacon." Or you can cook the bacon in the Instant Pot using the Sauté function.

1½ pounds boneless, skinless medium chicken breasts

Salt and ground black pepper

1 cup low-sodium chicken broth, homemade (see page 240) or store-bought

8 cups chopped romaine lettuce or spring mix

2 hard-boiled large eggs, sliced or diced

6 slices bacon, cooked and crumbled

1 cup halved cherry tomatoes

1 ripe avocado, sliced or diced

4 ounces Gorgonzola or feta cheese, crumbled

1½ cups Savory Cobb Vinaigrette (recipe follows)

Slow Cooker • MAKES: 4 ENTRÉE SALADS

MAKE IT NOW

1   Season the chicken generously on both sides with salt and pepper. *(Freezing instructions begin here.)*

2   Place the chicken in the slow cooker and pour in the broth.

3   Cover and cook on Low for 2½ to 3½ hours, until the chicken is cooked through. (The chicken is done when it is no longer pink inside and/or registers 165°F internally.)

4   Transfer the chicken to a cutting board and slice it into thin strips on an angle or chop into bite-size pieces.

5   Arrange the lettuce on a serving platter. Top with the chicken, eggs, bacon, tomatoes, avocado, and Gorgonzola. Shake up the vinaigrette and serve it alongside the salad.

FREEZE FOR LATER: Follow step 1. Place the seasoned chicken and the broth in a gallon-size freezer bag or container. Seal and freeze. Place the vinaigrette, bacon, and cheese in separate small freezer bags or containers. Seal and freeze alongside the chicken.

Note: You will need to have lettuce, hard-boiled eggs, cherry tomatoes, and avocado on hand to complete this meal. Thaw. Place in the slow cooker. Follow steps 3 through 5.

Instant Pot • MAKES: 4 ENTRÉE SALADS

MAKE IT NOW

1   Season the chicken generously on both sides with salt and pepper. *(Freezing instructions begin here.)*

2   Place the seasoned chicken in the 6-quart Instant Pot and pour in the broth. Lock and seal the lid. Cook at high pressure for 7 minutes, then quick release the pressure. (The chicken is done when it is no longer pink inside and/or registers 165°F internally.)

3   Transfer the chicken to a cutting board and slice it into thin strips on an angle or chop into bite-size pieces.

4   Arrange the lettuce on a serving platter. Top with the chicken, eggs, bacon, tomatoes, avocado, and Gorgonzola. Shake up the vinaigrette and serve it alongside the salad.

FREEZE FOR LATER: Follow step 1. Place the seasoned chicken and broth in a gallon-size freezer bag or round container (do not stack the chicken breasts in the bag/container; instead, place them side by side). Seal and freeze (if using a freezer bag, set it in a bowl or round container with a diameter similar to the Instant Pot so it will fit in the pot when frozen; see page 22). Place the vinaigrette, bacon, and cheese in separate small freezer bags or containers. Seal and freeze alongside the chicken.

PREPARE FROM FROZEN: *Note: You will need to have lettuce, hard-boiled eggs, cherry tomatoes, and avocado on hand to complete this meal.* Thaw the vinaigrette , bacon, and cheese. Set the Instant Pot to "Sauté." Transfer the frozen chicken to the pot and cook for 5 minutes to release some liquid. Press "Cancel." Follow step 2, but cook for 15 to 20 minutes. Follow steps 3 and 4.

(CONTINUES)

SAVORY COBB VINAIGRETTE

MAKES: ABOUT 1½ CUPS

¾ cup extra-virgin olive oil or avocado oil

6 tablespoons red wine vinegar

3 tablespoons freshly squeezed lemon juice (from about 1½ lemons)

1 tablespoon Dijon mustard

1 tablespoon organic or all-natural Worcestershire sauce

3 garlic cloves, minced

¾ teaspoon sugar

¾ teaspoon salt, plus more to taste

¾ teaspoon ground black pepper, plus more to taste

Combine all the ingredients in a mason jar with a lid or a quart-size freezer bag. Seal tightly and shake until combined. Taste and adjust the seasoning to your preference. This dressing can be stored in the refrigerator for up to 2 weeks or in the freezer for 3 to 6 months.

ASIAN SLAW WITH CHICKEN

You know that delicious slaw salad made with the prepackaged ramen noodles and seasoning packet? You know, the one full of processed ingredients and MSG? Well, we've reworked everybody's favorite slaw using ingredients you'll recognize. It's healthier than the original version and, in our opinion, even tastier! Serve it in the summer alongside corn on the cob and watermelon for a light picnic-style meal. The dressing would be delicious over stir-fried veggies or as a marinade for grilled chicken, too.

1½ pounds boneless, skinless medium chicken breasts

Salt and ground black pepper

1 cup low-sodium chicken broth, homemade (see page 240) or store-bought

½ cup slivered almonds

2 tablespoons hulled sunflower seeds

1 (16-ounce) package coleslaw mix, or 8 cups shredded cabbage

⅓ cup sliced green onions (about 3)

½ cup dried cranberries

½ cup frozen shelled edamame, thawed

1¼ cups Asian Sesame Dressing (recipe follows)

Slow Cooker • **MAKES: 4 OR 5 SERVINGS**

MAKE IT NOW

1   Season the chicken generously on both sides with salt and pepper. *(Freezing instructions begin here.)*

2   Place the seasoned chicken and broth in the slow cooker. Cover and cook on Low for 2½ to 3½ hours, until cooked through. (The chicken is done when it is no longer pink inside and/or registers 165°F internally.)

3   While the chicken cooks, preheat the oven to 350°F.

4   Place the almonds and sunflower seeds (if they aren't already toasted) on a rimmed baking sheet pan. Bake for 4 to 5 minutes, shaking the pan a few times, until lightly toasted and fragrant. Watch closely so they don't burn.

5   Transfer the chicken to a cutting board and chop into bite-size pieces.

6   In a large bowl, combine the chicken, almonds, sunflower seeds, coleslaw mix, green onions, cranberries, and edamame. About 30 minutes before serving, add about half the dressing and toss to coat. Serve the salad with the remaining dressing on the side.

(CONTINUES)

FREEZE FOR LATER: Follow step 1. Place the seasoned chicken and the broth in a gallon-size freezer bag or container. Seal and freeze. Preheat the oven to 350°F, follow step 4, then let the almonds and sunflower seeds cool. Place the almonds and sunflower seeds, cranberries, edamame, and dressing into separate small freezer bags or containers. Seal and freeze alongside the chicken.

PREPARE FROM FROZEN: *Note: You will need to have coleslaw mix and green onions on hand to complete this meal.* Thaw. Follow step 2. Then follow steps 5 and 6 to complete the salad.

Instant Pot • MAKES: 4 OR 5 SERVINGS

MAKE IT NOW

1   Season the chicken generously on both sides with salt and pepper. *(Freezing instructions begin here.)*

2   Place the seasoned chicken and the broth in the 6-quart Instant Pot. Lock and seal the lid. Cook at high pressure for 7 minutes, then quick release the pressure. (The chicken is done when it is no longer pink inside and/or registers 165°F internally.)

3   While the chicken cooks, preheat the oven to 350°F.

4   Place the almonds and sunflower seeds (if they aren't already toasted) on a rimmed baking sheet. Bake for 4 to 5 minutes, shaking the pan a few times, until lightly toasted and fragrant. Watch closely so they don't burn.

5   Transfer the chicken to a cutting board and chop into bite-size pieces.

6   In a large bowl, combine the chicken, almonds, sunflower seeds, coleslaw mix, green onions, cranberries, and edamame. About 30 minutes before serving, add about half the dressing and toss to coat. Serve the salad with the remaining dressing on the side.

FREEZE FOR LATER: Follow step 1. Place the seasoned chicken and the broth in a gallon-size freezer bag or round container (do not stack the chicken breasts in the bag/container; instead, place them side by side). Seal and freeze (if using a freezer bag, set it in a bowl or round container with a diameter similar to the Instant Pot so it will fit in the pot when frozen; see page 22). Preheat the oven to 350°F, follow step 4, and let the almonds and sunflower seeds cool. Place the

(CONTINUES)

almonds and sunflower seeds, cranberries, edamame, and dressing in separate small freezer bags or containers. Seal and freeze alongside the chicken.

PREPARE FROM FROZEN: *Note: You will need to have coleslaw mix and green onions on hand to complete this meal.* Thaw the nuts, cranberries, edamame, and dressing. Set the Instant Pot to "Sauté." Transfer the frozen meal to the pot and cook for 5 minutes to release some liquid. Press "Cancel." Follow step 2, but cook for 15 to 20 minutes. Then follow steps 5 and 6 to complete the salad.

ASIAN SESAME DRESSING
MAKES: 1¼ CUPS

½ cup peanut oil or avocado oil	¼ cup soy sauce	1 teaspoon sesame oil
⅓ cup rice vinegar	3 tablespoons honey	¼ teaspoon ground black pepper, plus more to taste

Combine all the ingredients in a mason jar with a lid or a quart-size freezer bag. Seal tightly and shake until combined. Taste and adjust the seasoning to your preference. This dressing can be stored in the refrigerator for up to 2 weeks or in the freezer for 3 to 6 months.

BALSAMIC STRAWBERRY AND CHICKEN SALAD

Prepare to be transported to a warm spring day as you enjoy this salad, which highlights spinach and strawberries. Creamy goat cheese, toasted sliced almonds, red onion, and sweet strawberries pair with the sweet-and-tangy balsamic dressing to top a bed of spinach. The added protein from the lean chicken breast makes this salad worthy of a light lunch or dinner any day of the week. A few other toppings that would work well are Mandarin orange segments, diced avocado, and blueberries.

1 to 1½ pounds boneless, skinless medium chicken breasts

Salt and ground black pepper

1 cup low-sodium chicken broth, homemade (see page 240) or store-bought

8 cups loosely packed baby spinach

½ cup sliced almonds or pecan halves, toasted

½ cup thinly sliced red onion

1 cup sliced fresh strawberries

4 ounces goat cheese or feta cheese, crumbled

1½ cups Honey Balsamic Vinaigrette (recipe follows)

Slow Cooker • MAKES: 4 ENTRÉE SALADS

MAKE IT NOW

1   Season the chicken generously on both sides with salt and pepper. *(Freezing instructions begin here.)*

2   Place the seasoned chicken and the broth in the slow cooker. Cover and cook on Low for 2½ to 3½ hours, until the chicken is cooked through. (The chicken is done when it is no longer pink inside and/or registers 165°F internally.)

3   Transfer the chicken to a cutting board and slice it into thin strips on an angle.

4   Arrange the spinach on a serving platter. Top with the chicken, almonds, onion, strawberries, and cheese. Shake up the vinaigrette and serve it alongside the salad.

(CONTINUES)

FREEZE FOR LATER: Follow step 1. Place the seasoned chicken and the broth in a gallon-size freezer bag or container. Seal and freeze. Place the vinaigrette, nuts, and cheese in separate small freezer bags or containers. Seal and freeze alongside the chicken.

PREPARE FROM FROZEN: *Note: You will need to have spinach, red onion, and strawberries on hand to complete this meal.* Thaw. Follow steps 2 through 4.

Instant Pot • MAKES: 4 ENTRÉE SALADS

MAKE IT NOW

1   Season the chicken generously on both sides with salt and pepper. *(Freezing instructions begin here.)*

2   Place the seasoned chicken and the broth in the 6-quart Instant Pot. Lock and seal the lid. Cook at high pressure for 7 minutes, then quick release the pressure. (The chicken is done when it is no longer pink inside and/or registers 165°F internally.)

3   Transfer the chicken to a cutting board and slice it into thin strips on an angle.

4   Arrange the spinach on a serving platter. Top with the chicken, almonds, onion, strawberries, and cheese. Shake up the vinaigrette and serve it alongside the salad.

FREEZE FOR LATER: Follow step 1. Place the seasoned chicken and the broth in a gallon-size freezer bag or round container (do not stack the chicken breasts in the bag/container; instead, place them side by side). Seal and freeze (if using a freezer bag, set it in a bowl or round container with a diameter similar to the Instant Pot so it will fit in the pot when frozen; see page 22). Place the vinaigrette, nuts, and cheese in separate small freezer bags or containers. Seal and freeze alongside the chicken.

PREPARE FROM FROZEN: *Note: You will need to have fresh spinach, red onion, and strawberries on hand to complete this meal.* Thaw the vinaigrette, nuts, and cheese. Set the Instant Pot to "Sauté." Transfer the frozen meal to the pot and cook for 5 minutes to release some liquid. Press "Cancel." Follow step 2, but cook for 15 to 20 minutes with a quick release. Follow steps 3 through 4.

HONEY BALSAMIC VINAIGRETTE

MAKES: ABOUT 1½ CUPS

¾ cup extra-virgin olive oil
or avocado oil

½ cup balsamic vinegar

¼ cup honey

1½ teaspoons salt, plus more
to taste

¾ teaspoon ground black
pepper, plus more to taste

Combine all the ingredients in a mason jar with a lid or a quart-size freezer bag. Seal tightly and shake until combined. Taste and adjust the seasoning to your preference. This dressing can be stored in the refrigerator for up to 2 weeks or in the freezer for 3 to 6 months.

ITALIAN HOUSE SALAD
WITH CHICKEN

At most family gatherings, my mom contributed a (huge!) version of a popular Italian restaurant's salad to go along with whatever the main dish was. It never stuck around for long. As a college student in my first apartment, I remember calling home to get the sacred recipe to make for my very first homemade dinner for friends. Fast-forward twenty years, and I'm so happy to be sharing a version of my family's recipe with you. Prep the simple components over the weekend and eat this delicious Mediterranean-influenced salad for days to come. —Rachel

1½ pounds boneless, skinless medium chicken breasts

Salt and ground black pepper

1 cup low-sodium chicken broth, homemade (see page 240) or store-bought

8 cups chopped romaine or green-leaf lettuce

1 cup sliced red onion

1 cup drained quartered artichokes hearts

1 cup pitted kalamata olives, halved

1½ cups Italian Parmesan Dressing (recipe follows)

Store-bought whole-grain or gluten-free croutons (optional)

Slow Cooker • MAKES: 4 ENTRÉE SALADS

MAKE IT NOW

1. Season the chicken generously on both sides with salt and pepper. *(Freezing instructions begin here.)*

2. Place the seasoned chicken and the broth in the slow cooker. Cover and cook on Low for 2½ to 3½ hours, until the chicken is cooked through. (The chicken is done when it is no longer pink inside and/or registers 165°F internally.)

3. Transfer the chicken to a cutting board and slice it into thin strips on an angle or chop into bite-size pieces.

4. Place the lettuce, chicken, onion, artichoke hearts, and olives in a large salad bowl. A few minutes before serving, shake up the dressing, pour the desired amount over the salad (start with ¼ cup), top with croutons, if desired, and toss. Serve the remaining dressing on the side.

FREEZE FOR LATER: Follow step 1. Place the seasoned chicken and the broth in a gallon-size freezer bag or container. Seal and freeze. Place the dressing in a separate small freezer bag or container. Seal and freeze alongside the chicken.

PREPARE FROM FROZEN: *Note: You will need to have lettuce, red onion, artichoke hearts, olives, and (optional) croutons on hand to complete this meal.* Thaw. Follow steps 2 through 4.

Instant Pot • MAKES: 4 ENTRÉE SALADS

MAKE IT NOW

1   Season the chicken generously on both sides with salt and pepper. *(Freezing instructions begin here.)*

2   Place the seasoned chicken and the broth in the 6-quart Instant Pot. Lock and seal the lid. Cook at high pressure for 7 minutes, then quick release the pressure. (The chicken is done when it is no longer pink inside and/or registers 165°F internally.)

3   Transfer the chicken to a cutting board and slice it into thin strips on an angle or chop into bite-size pieces.

4   Place the lettuce, chicken, onion, artichoke hearts, and olives in a large salad bowl. A few minutes before serving, shake up the dressing, pour the desired amount over the salad (start with ¼ cup), top with croutons, if desired, and toss. Serve the remaining dressing on the side.

FREEZE FOR LATER: Follow step 1. Place the seasoned chicken and the broth in a gallon-size freezer bag or round container (do not stack the chicken breasts in the bag/container; instead, place them side by side). Seal and freeze (if using a freezer bag, set it in a bowl or round container with a diameter similar to the Instant Pot so it will fit in the pot when frozen; see page 22). Place the dressing in a separate small freezer bag or container. Seal and freeze alongside the chicken.

PREPARE FROM FROZEN: *Note: You will need to have lettuce, red onion, artichoke hearts, olives, and (optional) croutons on hand to complete this meal.* Thaw the dressing. Set the Instant Pot to "Sauté." Transfer the frozen chicken to the pot and cook for 5 minutes to release some liquid. Press "Cancel." Follow step 2, but cook for 15 to 20 minutes. Follow steps 3 and 4.

(CONTINUES)

ITALIAN PARMESAN DRESSING

MAKES: ABOUT 1½ CUPS

⅔ cup extra-virgin olive oil

⅓ cup red wine vinegar

1 teaspoon salt, plus more to taste

½ teaspoon ground black pepper, plus more to taste

1 teaspoon sugar

3 garlic cloves, minced

⅔ cup grated Parmesan cheese

1 (4-ounce) jar diced pimientos, drained

Combine all the ingredients in a mason jar with a lid or a quart-size freezer bag. Seal tightly and shake until combined. Taste and adjust the seasoning to your preference. This dressing can be stored in the refrigerator for up to 2 weeks or in the freezer for 3 to 6 months.

HOMEMADE BBQ SAUCE

This easy BBQ sauce recipe is a combination of sweet-smoky-tangy flavors that can be adjusted to accommodate your preferences. Want it sweeter? Add more brown sugar or molasses. Want to skip the heat? Omit the red pepper flakes. We wrote this recipe to make 1½ cups because that's the amount called for by most of our recipes in this cookbook, but feel free to double, triple, or even quadruple it so you'll have plenty of sauce on hand when you need it. **MAKES: ABOUT 1½ CUPS**

½ cup cider vinegar

1 cup all-natural ketchup

3 tablespoons packed dark brown sugar

2 tablespoons molasses

1 teaspoon salt

1 teaspoon onion powder

¼ teaspoon dried mustard

¼ teaspoon red pepper flakes

¼ teaspoon ground black pepper

¼ teaspoon garlic powder

MAKE IT NOW: In a small saucepan, whisk together all the ingredients until well combined. Bring the mixture to a simmer over medium-high heat, stirring frequently so the bottom doesn't scorch. Reduce the heat to low and simmer, stirring occasionally, for 15 to 20 minutes, until the sauce has thickened.

FREEZE FOR LATER: Let the sauce cool completely. Pour it into a small freezer bag, mason jar, or freezer container. Seal and freeze. (If using a mason jar, be sure to leave at least 1 inch of headspace at the top.)

PREPARE FROM FROZEN: Thaw and use in recipes as directed.

Recipes That Use This Freezer Staple

Adelyn's Sticky BBQ Drumsticks *(page 57)*

Ultimate Chicken and Bacon Sandwiches *(page 94)*

Shredded BBQ Beef Sandwiches *(page 110)*

BBQ Pulled Pork Sandwiches *(page 148)*

BBQ Baby Back Ribs *(page 156)*

PESTO

Homemade pesto simply cannot be replicated! When basil is in season, it is totally worth taking the time to stock your freezer with pesto. Better yet, grow your own basil on the back porch in a pot and feel free to boast about your *truly* homemade pesto. **MAKES: 1 TO 1¼ CUPS**

2 cups packed fresh basil leaves

2 garlic cloves, peeled

¼ cup pine nuts or walnuts

½ cup freshly grated Parmesan cheese

½ cup extra-virgin olive oil, plus more for freezing

Salt and ground black pepper

MAKE IT NOW

1 In a food processor, combine the basil, garlic, nuts, and cheese. Pulse until coarsely chopped.

2 Add ½ cup olive oil and process until fully incorporated and smooth. Taste and season with salt and pepper.

FREEZE FOR LATER: *Note: You will need to have olive oil on hand.*

Option 1   Transfer the pesto to small, individual freezer containers and drizzle the remaining olive oil over the top to prevent browning. Seal tightly and freeze.

Option 2   Pour the pesto into an ice cube tray, drizzle with the remaining oil, and freeze until solid. Transfer the frozen pesto cubes to a freezer bag, seal, and freeze.

PREPARE FROM FROZEN: Thaw in the refrigerator. If using a pesto cube, place it in a small bowl first.

Recipes That Use This Freezer Staple

Mini Pesto Chicken Sammies *(page 97)*

Easy-Peasy Pesto Meatball Subs *(page 125)*

LOW-SODIUM CHICKEN BROTH

Any time you have leftover chicken parts, you have before you an opportunity to make chicken broth. Well, this recipe is really more of a stock because it's made with the bones rather than the meat, but stock and broth can be used interchangeably in our recipes. Not only do you save money by not buying the boxed stuff, but homemade broth is also so much healthier for you. Don't get too caught up in having the exact ingredients we've listed here, either. This recipe is a guideline of what you can put in your broth, but you can add or omit ingredients depending on what you have on hand. **MAKES: ABOUT 3 QUARTS (12 CUPS)**

Leftover chicken bones and carcass

1 onion, quartered

2 carrots, chopped into a few pieces

2 celery stalks, chopped into a few pieces

½ cup chopped fresh parsley

2 garlic cloves, peeled

1 teaspoon salt

1 teaspoon ground black pepper

MAKE IT NOW IN THE SLOW COOKER: Combine all the ingredients and 12 cups water in the slow cooker. Cover and cook on Low for 8 to 12 hours. Strain the broth, discarding the solids.

MAKE IT NOW IN THE INSTANT POT: Combine all the ingredients and 12 cups water in the Instant Pot. Lock and seal the lid. Cook at high pressure for 1 hour, then let the pressure release naturally. Strain the broth, discarding the solids.

FREEZE FOR LATER: Let the broth cool completely. Pour it into small freezer bags, mason jars, or freezer containers. (If using mason jars, be sure to leave at least 1 inch of headspace.) Label how much broth is in the bag or container (we recommend freezing it in 2-cup portions, since they're easier to thaw). Seal and freeze.

PREPARE FROM FROZEN: Thaw and use as needed.

TACO SEASONING

For years and years, I have been tripling or even quadrupling this recipe and storing it in a small mason jar alongside my other seasonings. If you carefully pour the seasonings in layer by layer, the colors are quite beautiful together and would even be a lovely gift. Just be sure to give it a good shake before using. —Polly

MAKES: GENEROUS ¼ CUP

1½ tablespoons chili powder

1 tablespoon ground cumin

1½ teaspoons salt

1½ teaspoons ground black pepper

¾ teaspoon garlic powder

¾ teaspoon onion powder

¾ teaspoon red pepper flakes

¾ teaspoon dried oregano

¾ teaspoon paprika

MAKE IT NOW: Combine all the ingredients in a small mason jar or freezer container. Seal and give it a good shake. Store in the pantry or freezer.

Recipes That Use This Freezer Staple

Cheesy Chicken Taquitos *(page 52)*

Fiesta Lime Chicken Bowls *(page 63)*

Baked Chicken and Black Bean Burritos *(page 76)*

Manchoes *(page 117)*

Shredded Beef and Cheese Taquitos *(page 142)*

Chicken Taco Soup *(page 174)*

Vegetarian Tortilla Soup *(page 199)*

Veggie-and-Bean-Stuffed Burritos *(page 219)*

RECIPE ICON INDEX

⌛ SLOW COOKS ALL DAY

👥 FEEDS A CROWD

❄ FULLY COOK AND FREEZE

"FULLY COOK AND FREEZE" RECIPE INSTRUCTIONS

Recipes that are marked "fully cook and freeze" (look for the ❄ icon) work well not only for family meals but also for individual lunches or dinners for just one or two people. These take a little more work on the front end but will stock up your freezer with healthy dishes that you can rewarm quickly on the back end. If a recipe doesn't instruct how to fully cook and freeze it, use these tips:

SHREDDED MEAT

▶ **TO FREEZE:** When the meat is done, use two forks to shred it, stir it back into the juices/sauce, and let cool completely. Either freeze the meat in its juices in individual portions or as a full meal using our freezing tips on page 19.

▶ **TO REHEAT:** Thaw. Rewarm in the slow cooker on Low, on the stovetop over low heat, or in the microwave, stirring occasionally, until warmed through.

MEATBALLS

▶ **TO FREEZE:** Let the meatballs cool completely. Freeze the meatballs in their sauce either in individual portions or as a full meal using our freezing tips on page 19.

▶ **TO REHEAT:** Thaw. Rewarm in the slow cooker on Low, on the stovetop over low heat, or in the microwave, stirring occasionally, until warmed through.

GROUND BEEF/CHICKEN/TURKEY

▶ **TO FREEZE:** Let the meat mixture cool completely. Freeze in individual portions or as a full meal using our freezing tips on page 19.

▶ **TO REHEAT:** Thaw. Rewarm in the slow cooker on Low, on the stovetop over low heat, or in the microwave, stirring occasionally, until warmed through. Serve as directed in the recipe.

SOUPS/STEWS/CHILIS/PASTA SAUCES

▶ **TO FREEZE:** When soup/stew/chili/pasta sauce is done, let it cool completely. Freeze either in individual portions or as a full meal using our freezing tips on page 19.

▶ **TO REHEAT:** *Option 1:* Thaw. Rewarm in the microwave, on the stovetop, or in the slow cooker until warmed through, stirring occasionally. *Option 2:* Set the Instant Pot to "Sauté." Transfer the frozen meal to the pot and cook for 5 minutes to release some liquid. Press "Cancel." Lock and seal the lid. Cook at high pressure for 5 minutes, then quick release the pressure. Stir. If not fully warmed through, cook for 1 to 2 minutes more.

BURRITOS

▶ **TO FREEZE:** Wrap individual burritos in foil and place them in a gallon-size freezer bag. Seal and freeze.

▶ **TO REHEAT:** *Option 1:* Remove the foil. Wrap one burrito in a moist paper towel. Microwave on high in 1-minute intervals. Flip the burrito after each, until warmed through on the inside. This will take about 2 to 3 minutes. *Option 2:* Place the frozen, foil-wrapped burrito in a preheated 400°F oven for 30 to 40 minutes, until heated through.

HOW TO KEEP YOUR FOOD SAFE

Here we've outlined the USDA's recommendations for minimum safe internal temperatures when cooking certain foods, as well as tips for safe serving and food storage.

SAFE COOKING TEMPERATURES

PRODUCT	TYPE	MINIMUM INTERNAL TEMPERATURE
Beef, Pork, Veal, and Lamb	Ground	160°F
	Steaks, chops, and roasts	145°F, plus rest for at least 3 minutes
Chicken and Turkey	Breasts	165°F
	Ground, stuffing, casseroles	165°F
	Whole bird, legs, thighs, wings	165°F
Eggs	Any	160°F
Fish and Shellfish	Any	145°F
Ham	Fresh or smoked (uncooked)	145°F, plus rest for at least 3 minutes
	Fully cooked (to reheat)	165°F
Leftovers	Any	165°F

SAFE SERVING AND FOOD STORAGE TIPS

▸ Hot food should be held at 140°F or warmer.

▸ Cold food should be held at 40°F or colder.

▸ Your refrigerator should be set at 40°F or lower and the freezer at 0°F or lower.

▸ Use most cooked leftovers within 3 to 4 days. (The USDA website has a thorough Cold Storage Chart with recommended storage times to help keep refrigerated and frozen foods safe.)

▸ Reheat leftovers to 165°F.

COOKING TIMES CHART FOR SLOW COOKER

Chicken	TIME
1 to 2 pounds medium-size boneless, skinless chicken breasts (seasoned or in sauce/marinade)	2½ to 3½ hours on Low
1 to 2 pounds boneless chicken thighs (seasoned or in sauce/marinade)	3 to 4 hours on Low
2½ to 3 pounds bone-in chicken thighs or drumsticks	3 to 4 hours on Low
Whole chicken (4 to 5 pounds)	4 to 6 hours on Low
Beef	
1 (approx. 3-pound) boneless beef chuck roast (seasoned or in sauce/marinade)	8 to 10 hours on Low or 5 to 6 hours on High
1 (approx. 3-pound) beef brisket, flat cut (seasoned or in sauce/marinade)	6 to 8 hours on Low
Ground beef	6 to 8 hours on Low
Ground beef, 2-inch meatballs	4 to 6 hours on Low
Pork	
1 (3- to 4-pound) pork shoulder	7 to 9 hours on Low or 4 to 5 hours on High
2½ to 3 pounds boneless pork loin	3 to 4 hours on Low
Soups	
Soup, with 1 to 2 pounds raw, boneless, skinless chicken breasts or thighs	4 to 6 hours
Soup, meatless	4 to 6 hours
Soup, ground beef, sausage, turkey, or bean-based	6 to 8 hours
Oats	
Steel-cut oats	6 to 8 hours

COOKING TIMES CHART FOR INSTANT POT

Chicken	FROM FRESH	FROM FROZEN*	RELEASE
1 to 2 pounds medium-size boneless, skinless chicken breasts (seasoned or in sauce/marinade)	7 minutes	15 to 20 minutes	Quick
1 to 2 pounds boneless chicken thighs (seasoned or in sauce/marinade)	7 minutes	15 to 20 minutes	Quick
2½ to 3 pounds bone-in chicken thighs or drumsticks	12 minutes	17 to 22 minutes	Quick
Whole chicken (4 to 5 pounds)	24 to 30 minutes	40 to 50 minutes (10 minutes per pound)	Natural
Beef			
1 (approx. 3-pound) boneless beef chuck roast (seasoned or in sauce/marinade), cut into 2x2-inch pieces	30 minutes	30 minutes	Natural
1 (approx. 3-pound) beef brisket, flat cut (seasoned or in sauce/marinade)	50 minutes	Not recommended	Natural
Ground beef	5 minutes	10 to 15 minutes	Quick
Ground beef, 2-inch meatballs	5 minutes	3 to 5 minutes	Quick
Pork			
1 (3- to 4-pound) pork shoulder, cut into four equal pieces	45 minutes	45 minutes	Natural
2½ to 3 pounds boneless pork loin	27 minutes	27 minutes (cut into three equal pieces)	Natural
Soups			
Soup, with 1 to 2 pounds raw, boneless, skinless chicken breasts or thighs	6 minutes	15 to 22 minutes (4 to 6 servings); 22 to 27 minutes (8+ servings)	Quick
Soup, meatless	7 to 10 minutes	12 to 17 minutes	Quick
Soup, ground beef, sausage, turkey, or bean-based	7 to 10 minutes	12 to 17 minutes	Quick
Oats			
Steel-cut oats	12 minutes	N/A	Natural

*We recommend sautéing frozen meals for 5 minutes first.

RECIPE CONTRIBUTORS

LIZ WEISS

Liz's Healthy Table, lizshealthytable.com
CONTRIBUTED: Barley and Chickpea Soup (page 204)

Liz Weiss, MS, RDN, is a mom of two grown boys with a specialty in family nutrition. She's the voice behind the family food podcast and blog *Liz's Healthy Table,* and her site is filled with easy, flavorful, and nourishing recipes that appeal to both kids and adults. Weiss has written several cookbooks, including the playful new coloring e-book series *Color, Cook, Eat!,* as well as *No Whine with Dinner* and *The Moms' Guide to Meal Makeovers.* Liz is a former producer and reporter for CNN and PBS HealthWeek and has appeared on national TV shows including the *TODAY* show, *Good Morning America,* and the *CBS Early Show.*

MOLLY STILLMAN

Still Being Molly, stillbeingmolly.com
CONTRIBUTED: Mouth-Watering Brisket with Balsamic Glaze (page 139)

Molly Stillman is the founder and creator of *Still Being Molly,* a life and style blog started in 2007, and the host of the *Business with Purpose* podcast. Her true passion lies in helping to inspire women to know that they were created on purpose, with a purpose, and for a purpose. Molly has had the honor of being featured in such publications and media as U.S. News & World Report, Scary Mommy, *The 700 Club,* and *Cary Magazine,* and was named as one of "The Carolinas 75 Most Stylish" by *Carolina STYLE Magazine.* She is a wife to John, mama to Lilly and Amos, dog mom to Tater and Audrey, a loud laugher, and a lover of Jesus, Diet Coke, and all the Chipotle burritos.

WHITNEY REIST

Sweet Cayenne, sweetcayenne.com
CONTRIBUTED: Zesty Italian Shredded Beef Subs (page 133)

Whitney Reist is a registered dietitian (RD) with professional culinary training who lives in the Nashville, Tennessee area with her husband, Ryan, who is also an RD. She has professional culinary training from Le Cordon Bleu and writes a food and lifestyle blog, *Sweet Cayenne,* where she loves to share wholesome recipes that focus on seasonal and high-quality ingredients. She is also very passionate about food-centered travel that involves experiencing new cultures through their local cuisine, and companion flower and vegetable gardening. She really enjoys documenting both of these pastimes on *Sweet Cayenne* from time to time.

KRISTIN SCHELL

The Turquoise Table, theturquoisetable.com
CONTRIBUTED: Pulled Pork Mojo Tacos (page 154)

Kristin Schell is on a mission to love her neighbors. She put a picnic table in her front yard, painted it turquoise, and began inviting neighbors, friends, and even strangers to hang out and do life together at the Turquoise Table. A gatherer at heart, Kristin brings people together for delicious food and stories at her table and her online home, *The Turquoise Table.*

ACKNOWLEDGEMENTS

If it weren't for the enthusiasm and support from our Thriving Home community of our first cookbook, *From Freezer to Table,* this one would not be in your hands today. Every recipe was created with you, our readers, in mind. Thank you for bringing a small piece of our hearts into your homes.

With the challenges that came with writing a cookbook like this, we are incredibly thankful for our official recipe testing team and other willing family, friends, and neighbors. They happily stepped into this journey with us, tested all sorts of (sometimes questionable) recipes, and took the time to offer constructive feedback. We couldn't have done this without their help!

We don't say it enough, but we are so grateful for the support from our husbands throughout this project. They were by our sides through every recipe success and failure. They helped us in many unseen ways as well: dishwashing, grocery shopping, vegetable chopping, and occasionally running out for takeout when a meal was an absolute bust. We are thankful to have them as unwavering teammates through the ups and downs of writing a cookbook.

We didn't know it at the time, but we struck gold when we signed on with our literary agent, Maria Ribas. Her perspective, guidance, and encouragement means the world to us as authors. We simply would not be where we are today without her.

There is a whole team of people who work hard behind the scenes to make a project like this come together. Much thanks to our Rodale team including Dervla Kelly (editor), Kim Tyner, Serena Wang, Mia Johnson, and many more who believe in this project and want to get it into the world as much as we do.

We had the amazing opportunity to see our photography team in action in Charleston, SC. Hélène, Tami, Angie, and Kelly were a well-oiled machine cranking out the most BEAUTIFUL food photos. We enjoyed watching and learning from them more than they will ever know.

Lastly, and most of all, we are grateful to the One who has called us to this crazy-fun-challenging job as cookbook authors. All good things come from His hand, and we see the gift of this book and our business as just that. May all we do be used to His glory and the good of many.

INDEX